Seeing Good At Work

Fifty-two Weekly Steps to Transforming Your Workplace Experience

Dr. Joyce Duffala and
Rev. Dr. Edward Viljoen

Science of Mind Publishing
Burbank, California

Science of Mind Publishing
2600 West Magnolia Boulevard
Burbank, California 91505-3031

Book design by Randall Friesen

Printed in the United States of America
ISBN: 0-9727184-3-5
Library of Congress Cataloging-in-Publication Data
Available Upon Request

Seeing Good At Work

With deep gratitude we honor and acknowledge
our teachers who have inspired us
and our loved ones who have supported us.

Special thanks to Randall Friesen,
whose commitment to this book
went beyond his role as publisher.

Contents

Introduction

WE WROTE THIS BOOK TO OFFER YOU WAYS OF SEEING AND EXPERIENCING more good in the workplace. Working on the principle that what you look for you will find, we believe that you can create a better experience for yourself at work by expanding your ability to look for good. As simple as it sounds, this is not necessarily an easy thing to accomplish. For many of us, it is *in* the workplace that we lose sight of goodness. What brings this about?

One factor is time pressure. When we move quickly, it is more difficult to be aware of how our thoughts, words, and actions affect us and those around us. We are then more likely to both initiate and fall prey to negativity.

A second factor concerns the high stakes involved in doing a good job at work. Salary increases, promotions, and even securing our current positions, are linked to the perception that we are doing a good job. This may cause us to feel frustrated and threatened when others seem to thwart our attempts at performing well.

The more we fear making a mistake, or performing poorly, or being taken advantage of, or losing our job, the more we can lose track of our own value and the value of those around us. Once fear takes hold, feelings of shame, acts of blame, and a culture of suspicion and isolation sets in. The more fearful we are, the more we tend to see things and people to be afraid of in the workplace.

This book was written to help you navigate through and out of the waters of stress and fear. Our compass has one direction: Look for the good around you. Look for good, and you will find it.

The principle that you find what you are looking for holds true on many levels. It is at work in the realm of quantum physics, where scientists have discovered that subatomic particles take on a specific form and location only when they are observed. The principle of finding what you are looking for is also responsible for the "placebo effect," long documented by medical professionals. And it shows up in the realm of human psychology, where our expectations shape our experience.

Our concept here is simple: Since what you look for you will find, look for good. But how do you put this simple concept into practice, especially in the demanding world of the workplace?

That is what this book is designed to do. Fifty-two short lessons—one per week—will give you ideas and exercises that strengthen your ability to see good in yourself, in others, and in your world.

The more good you are able to see, the more good you will experience. It is our hope that this book will help you lead a life of ever-expanding good, for yourself and others.

Joyce Duffala, Ed.D.
Edward Viljoen, R.Sc.F, D.D.

How To Use This Book

THERE IS GREAT POWER IN WRITING. WE INVITE YOU TO MAKE USE of this power when you use *Seeing Good At Work*. This book is interactive. To that end, we recommend you keep a notebook with you during your daily readings. Purchase the type of notebook you feel most comfortable with. Also keep a writing instrument, be it a pen or pencil or colored felt pen, close to your notebook. Making this process as easy as possible will keep you consistent on your pathway of discovery.

Each chapter of *Seeing Good At Work* contains an application exercise. The purpose of this exercise is to move the concepts of the chapter off the page and into your daily life. The application exercise usually involves a daily writing assignment or two. You should also use your notebook to record any observations, discoveries, questions, thoughts, or feelings you have about the week's topic each day. When you reach the beginning of the next week, wherever you are on your notebook page, turn it and begin on a fresh, clean page and write the new week number at the top.

At the end of each chapter, you will find a short "Remind Yourself" statement that you can memorize and repeat to yourself throughout the week. These affirmative statements, along with your daily writings, will bring the lessons of *Seeing Good At Work* more powerfully into your life.

You might also consider going through the material in this book with a friend or small study group. In this way, you can share insights and growth, and support each other in seeing good at work.

Do you know what astonished me the most in this world?
The inability of force to create anything.
In the long run, the sword is always beaten by the spirit.
—Napoleon Bonaparte

Week 1
Questioning Your Reactions

"Nothing's good nor bad but thinking makes it so."
—William Shakespeare

HAVE YOU EVER NOTICED HOW BABIES AND VERY SMALL CHILDREN experience an injury, react to it, and then move on to the next adventure with the adverse event forgotten? Such minimal reactions to a physical injury can amaze adults who might expect the child to respond in quite a different way.

As we grow older, we are more apt to judge things as "bad" or "good." Over time, when something "bad" happens, our reactions become stronger, and we hold on to them longer, as they carry with them memories of a history of past hurts. In this way, we pass from the realm of purely physical reaction into the realm of memory reaction, associating with the memory of what is bad.

This is where we find ourselves as adults, mentally carrying around a detailed list of good things and bad things. And as we go through our daily lives, we continue to judge the things in our lives as either good or bad.

But what if we realized our judgments were arbitrary? It is an observable fact that what some call bad, others call good. Could it be that a bad experience is uncomfortable because of how we are thinking about it, and what it reminds us of? Is it possible that we could change the experience if we were able to change our thoughts about it?

This first lesson challenges you to consider the possibility that there is indeed a relationship between thought and experience. As you go through the week, note your negative reactions, and consider an alternative response.

Application Exercise

1. Start your *Seeing Good At Work* notebook today. Each week, begin by writing the week number at the top of the page. For example, today you will write "Week 1."
2. Next, begin two lists for this week's application exercise. One is "Things I Like" and the other is "Things I Don't Like." Each day this week, take two minutes to look around and identify things that please you and things that don't please you, and list them under these headings.
3. Remembering Shakespeare's quote that "nothing's good nor bad but thinking makes it so," look at your list. For each item you've written, say to yourself, "I have chosen to like/not like ________________________."
4. Throughout the week, whenever you notice yourself labeling something or someone as bad, gently ask yourself the question: Is there any other way I could be thinking or feeling now?

Remind Yourself

I CHOOSE MY REACTIONS TO PEOPLE AND EVENTS.

Week 2
Watch Your Mouth!

"Your word is powerful. Choose it wisely."
—Adapted from Native American wisdom

OUR SENSES TAKE IN ZILLIONS OF PIECES OF INFORMATION. Naturally, we are not consciously aware of all of them—most go unnoticed. So how is it that we "decide" which ones we pay attention to?

To a great extent, our language defines what we notice in our environment and what we ignore. For example, the wine connoisseur's vocabulary allows her to note and enjoy a wide bouquet of flavors and nuances that most of us do not experience. Linguists describe how people of different cultures live in realities shaped by their language. English speakers perceive a world defined and delineated by English. Speakers of other languages see the world a bit differently, based on the structure and vocabulary of their language.

This linguistic principle points to an important element in our everyday lives: When we talk about something, we bring it more fully to our attention. The more we speak about something, the more it commands our attention, and the more it will influence our experience.

This principle applies not only to what we say, but also to what we spend time listening to others say, either in conversations, on television or radio, or through the print media.

It also means we can begin to shape our experience by taking control of what we say, as well as what we absorb through listening and reading. As we increase the amount of time spent talking about positive things and decrease the amount of time complaining about negative things, we shift the focus of our minds and of our experience in a positive direction. Similarly, spending time with people who have a positive take on most situations—rather than those who predict the worst—will uplift our mood and experience. This holds true for everything we absorb, from the kind of news reporting we watch to the type of novels we read.

This week, take the first step in changing your experience for the better by becoming aware of exactly what you are paying attention to through the use of your own words and through what you are listening to.

Application Exercise

1. At the end of each day this week, take a moment to write in your notebook the three things you spent the most time talking about during the day. Note, too, any emotional qualities associated with these topics (such as frustration, enthusiasm, or some other emotion).
2. Next, ask yourself whether or not there is any connection between what you spent your time talking about and the things that happened to you. Write down the thoughts that come to mind.

Remind Yourself

I consciously choose what I speak about and listen to.

Week 3
Avoiding Assumptions

"Never attribute to intention that which can be attributed to ignorance."
—Contemporary Wisdom

AN OLD ADAGE WARNS THAT WHEN YOU "ASSUME," YOU MAKE AN "ass" out of "u" and "me." Sometimes it is easier to assume than to take the steps required to find definitive answers. Making assumptions can become a habit of purposely "not knowing." At worst, it can increase the sense of separation and isolation in a workplace in which everyone assumes that everyone else is doing what ought to be done.

Assumptions can be particularly damaging when we have been previously hurt, when we leap to the conclusion that the "attack" was purposeful—even premeditated. If we follow the standard "lazy" method of accepting this assumption, we risk establishing a long-term, widening breach with the person involved.

Perhaps you have occasionally summoned up your courage to speak to the "perpetrator" of your injury, only to find that he or she had no idea of your response, and in fact had no intention of hurting you at all. Actually, his or her attention in the situation was on something completely apart from you.

When this happens, it serves as a reminder that any act, any situation, any word has numerous interpretations. You are always at choice as to what your interpretation is. It also serves to remind you that the only way to truly know what others are thinking—what their motives or intentions are—is to ask them. This requires true openness. It requires you to set aside blame in the quest of understanding the other's point of view. And, more importantly, it results in replacing assumptions with facts and an improved understanding of the situation. In the best case, you discover your hurt was unnecessary. In the worst, you know where you stand.

Application Exercise

1. Make two lists in your notebook this week: "Incident" and "Possible Explanations." Under the first list, write down an incident in which you were hurt that day. Under the second, list as many possible reasons you can imagine for why the person did it, other than trying to hurt you.
2. Talk to at least one of the people you listed above about the incident. Ask if your understanding of the situation matches his or hers.

Remind Yourself

I AM EXPANDING MY AWARENESS OF OTHER PEOPLE'S POINTS OF VIEW.

Week 4

Listening for Good

"May I not so much seek...to be understood, as to understand."
—St. Francis of Assisi

THERE IS A CARTOON STRIP IN WHICH A LITTLE GIRL LOOKS UP AT her father who is reading the newspaper. She says to him, "Dad, you have to listen to me with your eyes as well as your ears." In a busy workplace, it is possible to fall into the habit of listening with only one ear and a minimum of attention. Someone once observed that most people in a conversation are not listening; they are merely waiting for their chance to speak.

Consider this idea: hearing the words and understanding them is not always enough to "catch" what a person is communicating to you. Listening is more than the physical process of receiving aural information. It is even more than a mental process of interpreting and analyzing the information being received. Listening, true listening, must include a relationship, an interaction between the listener and the speaker. It requires eyes, ears, and attention.

A good listener is a good receiver. A good receiver has to be wide open to the entire communication process. When you become sincerely willing to hear, you discover a whole new world of understanding. You will find that people are telling you so much more than words. Hidden within their sentences are clues about how to do better, where to get help, and what is important in the world. Your job is to move from waiting for your turn to talk to the place of really, truly listening.

If you have poor listening skills with others, it could be that you have the same poor skills in hearing the messages and information that your own inner life is constantly giving you. As you improve one, the other also improves.

Application Exercise

1. Make two lists for this week: "I Listen Attentively When..." and "My Attention Wanders When... ." Each day this week, write down instances in which you were listening fully to another person and instances where you noted that you were not.
2. Write suggestions to yourself as to how you can listen better.
3. This week, when anyone attempts to communicate with you, stop what you are doing and listen with your eyes, ears, and attention. If you have anything in your hands, put it down. If you are engaged in another activity, take a moment to note where you are, and pause so that you can return to it later. Practice giving your full and undivided attention to people who are communicating with you. When they have finished speaking, repeat back to them what you heard. Ask if you understood correctly.

Remind Yourself

WHEN I AM WILLING TO REALLY LISTEN,
I OPEN MYSELF TO A NEW WORLD OF UNDERSTANDING.

Week 5
Accepting and Releasing Your Mistakes

"Mistakes are part of the dues one pays for a full life."
—Sophia Loren

HAVE YOU EVER NOTICED THAT YOUR MISTAKES FREQUENTLY SEEM larger to you than to others? I noticed this recently when I performed some music and made what I considered to be two rather serious mistakes. My embarrassment eased as person after person congratulated me on my performance. Gradually, I was comforted by the awareness that they hadn't even noticed my errors.

We tend to be ashamed of our mistakes, but mistakes are necessary in learning. Not only do we learn from our mistakes, but in order to learn, we *must* make mistakes. I have a friend who falls down every time he goes cross-country skiing, because he always tries something new. On a day when he does not fall, he knows he has only used the old, familiar techniques and has not stretched himself to a new level of learning and competence.

We begin our lives knowing this. Toddlers learning to walk simply get back up after they fall down. Yet somewhere along the line, we develop a sense of shame when making mistakes, focusing more on the error than on the gift of knowledge contained in the experience. A South African proverb reminds us: "Don't look where you fell; look where you tripped."

We have come to expect perfection of ourselves, even when we try something new. This is extremely limiting. We rob ourselves of the joy of exploring new things when we fear making mistakes and expect ourselves to be flawless. Here, the words of the Rev. Linda McNamar can help: "We come to the threshold of wisdom within us as we begin to accept ourselves, not as imperfect, but as perfectly human rather than humanly perfect."

Application Exercise

1. This week, when you do something that you consider to be a mistake, write it in your notebook.
2. Next, rate each mistake on a scale of 1 to 10 (low to high) based on the following questions:
   How important is this to me?
   How important is this to other people?
   How important will this be in 5 years?
3. Write down any advice to yourself you learned from this incident (e.g., "In the future I will remember that…").
4. On a separate piece of paper, make a note of your mistake. When finished, toss the piece of paper into a wastepaper basket as you say out loud, "I am perfectly human. I release this mistake with gratitude for the wisdom it has brought me."

Remind Yourself

I ACCEPT EACH MISTAKE AS A NATURAL STEP IN LEARNING AND GAINING WISDOM. I LEARN FROM MY MISTAKES AND MOVE ON.

Week 6
What's Right?

"The greater part of our happiness or misery depends on our dispositions and not on our circumstances."
—Martha Washington

WHEN WE ARE IN DIFFICULT OR CHALLENGING SITUATIONS, THERE is a natural tendency for the mind to focus on what is wrong. It is not unlike stubbing a toe, when, for several seconds, the painful toe seems to be all that exists. We might be in one of our favorite places on a beautiful day, yet the pain seems to obliterate all else around us.

Another mental tendency in difficult situations is to extrapolate from the present and imagine the worst-case scenario. Why is this an important thing to note? In the past few years, quantum scientists have observed that people's expectations have an effect on the physical world. It is also well established that there is a "law of expectations" at work in experiments involving placebos. This evidence suggests that we find what we expect to find; what we end up with in a situation is determined by what we decided to look for in the first place.

Let us speculate how this law of expectations works in a challenging situation. If we expect bad things to happen, chances are they will. If we expect good things to happen, chances are they will. Couple with this another principle, that what you place your attention on will expand in your experience, and there seems to be a pretty good case for finding what is right in any situation.

That is the invitation of this week's lesson—to look for what is right, particularly in what appear to be challenging situations. We are not suggesting that you delude yourself about all the things that are wrong or that may go wrong; this would seem illogical and unsatisfying. We simply suggest that you *additionally* look for what is right.

Experience proves that this simple exercise, done consistently and over time, brings about a steady increase in the good one experiences in life.

Application Exercise

If you experience a challenging situation this week, make a note of it in your notebook. Then, answer the following questions:

1. What is wrong with this situation?
2. What is the worst thing that could happen?
3. What one thing, if changed, would make all the difference in this situation?
4. What can I do to encourage this change? Is it the right thing to do?
5. What is right or good in this situation?
6. What are some possible positive outcomes?
7. What can I do to increase what is positive or good in this situation?

Remind Yourself

THERE IS ALWAYS MORE RIGHT THAN WRONG IN ANY SITUATION.

Week 7
Accepting Compliments

"I can live for two months on a good compliment."
—Attributed to Mark Twain

MANY OF US WERE RAISED WITH THE IDEA THAT IT IS GOOD TO BE modest. This includes dismissing, diminishing, or even negating statements we receive as compliments. How often do we find ourselves saying things like, "Oh, this old thing. I just threw it on," or "Well, I couldn't have done it without the rest of my team."?

As noble as this might seem at first, dismissing compliments can be a disservice both to the person giving the compliment and to you.

By giving a compliment, the compliment-giver is actually offering you a gift. By not accepting it, you rob him of the pleasure of giving. If you deflect or negate a compliment with your own thoughts or words, you may be going beyond the merely ungenerous act of not receiving the gift to that of literally accusing the other person of being wrong or lying.

Even more problematic is the message you give yourself. Each time you refuse a compliment, you essentially tell yourself you are not good, not worthy of such praise. And when you have done this for many years, the story becomes quite convincing!

The good news is that it is possible to reverse this pattern. Start today by simply saying "Thank you" when someone gives you a compliment. Receive the compliment as the gift it was intended to be. Think about it. Write the compliment down. Repeat it to yourself as often as necessary until you, like the person who gave it, believe it to be true.

P.S. If you find this week that you are not receiving any compliments, you can start the flow by giving a few of them!

APPLICATION EXERCISE

1. Each day this week, make a note of any compliments you received. Write down the compliment and the person who gave it.
2. Then answer the following questions for each compliment you have written down:
   What does this compliment tell me about myself?
   What does it tell me about the person who gave it to me?
3. This week, whenever you are paid a compliment, simply say, "Thank you." Silently add the words in your mind: "It's really true!"

REMIND YOURSELF

I UPLIFT BOTH MYSELF AND OTHERS
BY GRACEFULLY ACCEPTING COMPLIMENTS.

Week 8
Taking Charge: Making Small, Positive Changes

"Each of us can work to change a small portion of events and in the total of all of those acts will be written the history of this generation."
—Robert Kennedy

FROM TIME TO TIME I FEEL AN ODD BUT FAMILIAR CONFLICT RISE up in me at work. I want everyone to accept me "just the way that I am," while at the same time I want everyone to "expect the best of me." It is not that I want to stay the way I am; I want to improve. It is just that I also don't want to change.

At times like this, I remind myself of the phrase, "If you continue to do what you've always done, you will continue to have what you've always had. If you *do* different, you will *have* different." I appreciate this piece of wisdom because it reminds me that mastering life in the workplace is not a mystery reserved for an elite few. It reminds me that I can effectively change my life at work by using a simple, everyday resource: my natural ability to change.

I know that if I find myself feeling stuck or frustrated in a situation, I can begin the powerful process of transformation with the simple question: "What can I do today to make my life better?" Then I observe the first spontaneous answer that comes to mind. The answer does not have to relate to the frustration I feel, nor must it have anything to do with work. I just ask the question. Then, if possible at that time, I take the necessary steps to do that thing to make my life better.

Action is the antidote to depression, confusion, and anger, as well as the key to unlocking creative thought. Action creates the vital energy of self-esteem. Too often, however, we think about making changes rather than actually making them.

In his book *Life Strategies*, Dr. Phillip McGraw writes about making changes: "If the people around you cannot observe, from their external vantage point, that you are behaving differently, then you are falling short… . You must be willing to change the direction in your life. In order to do that, you must reorganize yourself and your day in a way that moves you up the performance ladder. Believe me, performance is contagious. If you begin to do some things differently, this will stimulate additional changes."

Application Exercise

1. Take a moment each day to answer the following question: "What one thing can I do to make my life better?" Write in your notebook whatever answer comes spontaneously into your mind. Do not edit or question the relevance of the thought, just write it down.
2. Next, write a list of the benefits this change could cause in your life, and write down the date by which you will accomplish each item. You can follow these guidelines:
   a. One thing I can do to make my life better is:
   b. This change could cause the following benefits in my life:
   c. The date by which I commit to make this change is:

Remind Yourself

I AM AN EFFECTIVE, CREATIVE, AND
INTELLIGENT AGENT FOR CHANGE IN MY LIFE.

Week 9
Are You Blessing Or Cursing?

"Your attitude is independent of circumstances. It comes from your own self talk."
—Dr. Michael Beckwith

IN WEEK 2, WE CONSIDERED THAT WHAT YOU TALK ABOUT REVEALS what you pay attention to, and likewise what you create in your experience. Simply put, the more we talk about something, the more we bring it into our awareness, and the more we bring it into our experience.

This week, we put our attention on *how* we speak about things, for how we speak about things will determine the quality of our experience.

If we speak well of something—that is, if we "bless" it—then we emphasize good in our awareness and in our continued experience of that thing.

If we speak ill of something—that is, if we "curse" it—then we emphasize negativity in our awareness and invite a continued negative experience of that thing. This simple principle applies equally to events, objects, and people: how we describe them shapes how we will experience them.

The good news is that if we want to change our experience of an event, object, or person, an effective first step is to take control of how we speak about it.

You can start this process right now by becoming aware of how you speak about things, noting whether you are "blessing" or "cursing" experiences and people in your life. Once you do this, decide if you would like to alter your experience by altering your words.

Application Exercise

1. Make two lists in your notebook for this week: "Things I Have 'Blessed' With My Words Today" and "Things I Have 'Cursed' With My Words Today." Each day this week, write down the corresponding events under each heading.
2. At the end of the week, choose one of the things you have "cursed," and write something good about it. For example, if you talked about how a co-worker is stubborn, you might write a sentence or two about his or her good qualities. ("He takes his work very seriously." "She always follows through.")

Remind Yourself

By speaking of good, I bless my life and bring more good into my awareness and experience.

Week 10

What Are You Telling Yourself?

"If you think you can or you think you can't, you're right."
—Henry Ford

THE COMMENTS AND CRITICISM WE RECEIVED WHEN WE WERE young greatly affect our self-image and sense of self-esteem today. Yet those remarks were made a long time ago. Now the important thing is what we tell ourselves about ourselves in each moment.

There are many reasons for giving ourselves more negative messages than positive, uplifting ones. Perhaps we think we should not be boastful, even when talking to ourselves. Perhaps we are repeating what was said to us early on in our lives. Perhaps we think if we put ourselves down first, it will stop other people from doing so. Maybe we even think that, by saying shaming things to ourselves, we are moving forward on the road of self-improvement.

However, what we think and say to ourselves does become true in our experience. If we repeatedly focus on our faults, we will indeed experience them more consistently. Sally Kempton captured the damaging effects of this tendency when she said, "It is hard to fight an enemy who has outposts in your own head."

Fortunately, the opposite is also true. If we repeatedly dwell on our good points, then this awareness will create increasing good in our experience of ourselves.

Cultural anthropologist Angeles Arrien recounts how many indigenous people daily pose this question: "Is my self-worth as strong as my self-critic? And if I can answer yes to that question, then I am ready to face the gift of this day. Then I know I am honoring the gems, the treasure jewels, the pearls within as much as I'm honoring the beast within." Begin this week to honor the good of who you are, for as you applaud your good qualities, you encourage their expansion and growth.

Application Exercise

1. At the start of each day, write two positive, encouraging things to say to yourself.
2. At the end of each workday, take a moment to reflect on what you said to yourself about yourself throughout the day. In your notebook, keep track of those things by listing them under the following headings:
   Positive, encouraging things I said to myself.
   Negative, shaming things I said to myself.

Remind Yourself

BY SPEAKING WELL OF MYSELF TO MYSELF, I INCREASE MY CAPACITY FOR SUCCESS, FULFILLMENT, AND HAPPINESS.

Week 11
Being Grateful, Part I

"It's such a wonderful feeling to be thankful. It prepares and opens the way for more good to come into our lives."
—Louise L. Hay

GRATITUDE IS THE ACT OF ACKNOWLEDGING AND BEING THANKFUL for the good you have experienced. Expressing gratitude is one of the most accessible and beneficial ways of creating more good in your life. We will focus on this simple but powerful method for transformation in the next two weeks.

Gratitude works on two levels—the level of thought and the level of feeling. This week we will consider the thought level of gratitude.

To use gratitude on a level of thought, simply make note of all the things, people, and events in your life (past or present) that you appreciate and enjoy. This is hardly a new technique, as no doubt someone in your life has advised you at some point to "count your blessings." What we suggest here is that you begin to discipline your mind to do this on a regular basis. This simple act is a definite way to increase your experience of good in your life.

Why does such a simple method have such a powerful effect? One reason is that by focusing your thought on what you appreciate, you bring attention to the good in your life. The more you look at your life with an attitude of gratitude, the more you increase your awareness of those things in your life for which to be grateful, as well as your ability to see good.

Some days, though, can be unpleasant and difficult. If you have had what you deem a "bad day," we suggest that you nonetheless (and perhaps, especially) go through this exercise of noting what is good in your life. You may find yourself relying on some small detail (your nail polish or socks) or something that is commonly present (the comfort of your chair or the gentleness of a breeze). Over time, this discipline has the powerful effect of allowing you to see good in any situation.

Begin this week to make note of the good in your life. You will soon find that you have more and more for which to be grateful.

Application Exercise

1. Each morning as soon as you wake up, immediately think of three things for which you are grateful.
2. At the end of each workday, write down five things for which you are grateful at work—either things in general or things that specifically transpired during that day.

Remind Yourself

I HAVE MANY THINGS FOR WHICH TO BE GRATEFUL.

Week 12
Being Grateful, Part II

"A grateful mind is a great mind which eventually attracts to itself great things."
—Plato

LAST WEEK WE CONSIDERED GRATITUDE ON THE LEVEL OF thought. This week we look at gratitude on the level of feeling.

Developing your feeling of gratitude is equally important to last week's regimen of training your thought to focus on gratitude. Feelings work much like thoughts when it comes to creating our future. Just as that which we now think about focuses our attention, shapes our expectations, and creates our future experience, so it is with feelings. A feeling of happiness creates a mental atmosphere that invites more happiness into our lives. A feeling of gratitude literally attracts more for which to be grateful.

We usually think of feelings as being a result of or a reaction to events in our lives. For example, someone gives you a compliment, and you feel happy. What we suggest here, however, is that it is possible to experience feelings without a specific external stimulus. It is possible to feel gratitude without having an "excuse" to be grateful.

To do this, simply remember what it felt like when you were grateful for something in the past, or imagine what it would feel like to receive a gift for which you have been waiting. As you do so, notice the state of mind and body you assume. With a little practice, you will soon be able to re-create this state and immerse yourself in the feeling of gratitude for no reason at all. Try it right now. Close your eyes for a moment, and imagine you are feeling grateful.

Plato, who spoke of the connection between gratefulness and greatness, pointed out the benefits of this discipline some 2,400 years ago. It is a discipline that we encourage you to begin this week and continue for the rest of your life—a life filled with ever-expanding good both inside and outside of the workplace.

Application Exercise

1. As you did last week, each morning as soon as you awake, immediately think of three things for which you are grateful.
2. Twice during your workday—once in the morning and once in the afternoon—pause for a moment and assume the feeling of gratitude. This is a time to feel grateful without bringing to mind any specific thing for which you are grateful. Simply let a feeling of gratitude infuse your body, mind, and soul. At the end of your workday, note any observations you have about this gratitude practice.
3. Create a gratitude journal to keep at your bedside. Each night before sleeping, note at least five things for which you are grateful. These can be specific events from the day, or things that are present in your life in general. This is the beginning of a practice that will continue in weeks and months to come.

Remind Yourself

I constantly feel grateful.

Week 13

Staying Conscious and Present All Day

"That the birds of worry and care fly above your head, this you cannot change, but that they build nests in your hair, this you can prevent."
—Chinese Proverb

MUCH HAS BEEN WRITTEN ABOUT THE VALUE OF LIVING IN THE present moment. When we are in the mental state of being present—living in the moment—we are most effective and most alive. When we are fully aware of what is going on around us, we are able to give and receive the most life has to offer.

But what a difficult thing it can be to do! Our attention is usually on something that happened in the past, something that may transpire in the future, or other imaginary scenarios—both pleasant and unpleasant. This age-old struggle is compounded in this electronic age with its myriad distractions. The popularity of the phrase "be here now" attests to the fact that this is a special challenge for our time.

There are many experiences that can pull you out of the present moment. One is feeling overwhelmed by your daily tasks—that nagging feeling that, in addition to what you are involved in right now, there are other incomplete tasks looming on the horizon. Heightened by the urgency of deadlines, "task overwhelm" can lead to a panicky, "out of body" sensation. Again, this problem is compounded by the technology of our age, an age in which computers, e-mail, and voice mail have no built-in activity/rest cycles, but rather impart work demands twenty-four hours a day.

The physical environment of the workplace may also affect our ability to be present. Uncomfortable furniture, stale air, or poor lighting can make your attempts at being present more difficult. Added to this are numerous visual and sound stimuli simultaneously vying for your attention.

Your internal state—both physical and emotional—affects your presence of mind. Being tired, hungry, hot, or ill detracts from your mental presence. Negative emotions also diminish your ability to be present. Fear, shame, and self-consciousness may bring about a desire to escape from what is going on in the moment.

Another factor is the thought or feeling that you could be doing something better than what you are doing now—something more exciting, something more pleasant, something more worthwhile. This attitude diminishes both the potential and the enjoyment of the moment.

Deepak Chopra believes "there is no higher purpose than trying to open your awareness until the full impact of reality—in all its beauty, truth, wonder, and sacredness—is consciously experienced." Begin this week by encouraging yourself to be as present as possible in all that you are doing.

Application Exercise

Throughout the day, notice when you are present and when you are not present in what you are doing. Each day, take a few minutes to note those times by answering the following questions in your notebook:

1. When was I most fully present in what I was doing?
2. When I noticed that I was not present in what I was doing, what were the reasons?
3. What can I do in the future to change these reasons so I can be more fully present?
4. What is the value for me of being present?

Remind Yourself

I OPEN MYSELF TO THE FULLNESS OF LIFE IN THIS MOMENT.

Week 14
Organizing Your Mind for Peace and Performance

"Order is Heaven's first law."
—Alexander Pope

ANXIETY, WHICH MAY STEM FROM THE FEELING OF BEING OVER-whelmed with things to do, can make it difficult to observe and experience the good in and around us. We can address this by working with the idea that the feeling of anxiety is based on a perception, and that any perception is simply a thought. What if, through changing the thought, we could change the perception? What if, through changing the perception, we could change the feeling and the experience?

Since the mind works very quickly, we can easily become overwhelmed by the quantity of thoughts and perceptions we experience in a short span of time. The numerous thoughts that pass through our minds each second do not occur in a linear, logical fashion, but in an organic, diffuse way. So as you begin to think about your day, your mind might literally jump from one thought to the next, from one item on your "to do" list to the next. This can lead to the feeling that you have too much to handle.

One remedy lies in passing these amorphous, spread-out thoughts through a filter of orderliness. This can be accomplished by making a list of everything you need to do whenever you feel overwhelmed, and then prioritizing the tasks by their importance.

This simple act has the power to impart a feeling of relief and a sense of control. It also frees up creative mental resources. Once your thoughts are safely down on paper, you can trust they will not be forgotten. Your mind no longer has to worry about trying to remember a lot of details. It can get busy doing what it does best—creative problem solving and strategizing about the tasks themselves.

Note, too, that you can receive these mental benefits even if you do not actually accomplish the tasks you have written down. The point is that when you observe what is on your mind—when you read what you have written down—you will attain focus, calm, and order.

At the end of your day, you can decide which unfinished items move to tomorrow's list. Or, you may want to start a new list if you find that helpful. You may even find that some items on your list no longer seem urgent or even necessary.

This technique works whenever you start to feel overwhelmed. Simply take a moment to write down your tasks. Seeing them organized on paper will restore a feeling of order, peace, and control.

Application Exercise

1. At the beginning of each day, list the tasks you have to accomplish. Then, re-order them according to priority.
2. During the day, anytime you are feeling overwhelmed, take a moment to write down the tasks on your mind. Note which items need specific action.
3. At the end of the day, reflect for a moment on how listing and prioritizing your tasks and thoughts may have brought a greater feeling of order and peace. Record your observations in your notebook.

Remind Yourself

BY BRINGING ORDER TO MY CREATIVITY,
I INCREASE MY PEACE, PERFORMANCE, AND PRODUCTIVITY.

Week 15
Relaxation and Centering

"The more peace you have in your own life the more you can reflect into your surroundings, and ultimately into your world."
—Peace Pilgrim

THE PHYSIOLOGICAL AND MENTAL BENEFITS OF RELAXATION ARE well documented. There is no doubt that taking time to relax during the day is healthy for the body and allows the mind to work better. Every organ, system, and function of the body and mind benefits when you release tension and return to a physically balanced state.

But how easily the day overtakes us! Too frequently, any relaxed feeling we may have had when walking into work swiftly becomes a distant memory. Time passes quickly, and it is easy, when faced with the immediate demands and pressures of our jobs, to overlook our good intentions of taking a moment to rejuvenate ourselves.

The good news is that the act of relaxation need not be time-consuming. You do not have to change your environment or routine in any extraordinary way. Relaxation can occur in a very ordinary and brief act known as *centering*.

Centering is simply taking a moment to "come back to yourself," regardless of where you are or what you are doing. It is helpful anytime you are in a difficult situation. One easy and ancient way to center is to pay attention to your breath. Take a moment right now to pause and close your eyes. Inhale, hold the breath for a moment, exhale and mentally count "1." Now inhale, hold the breath, exhale and mentally count "2." Continue until you have completed 10 breaths.

Doing this once an hour can help release tension and pressure, oxygenate your body, and increase mental clarity and productivity. Since you must stop all other activity to do it, you also change the pace of your day. And most importantly in our busy world, taking a moment to center does not consume a lot of time—probably the same amount of time it would take to complain about being overwhelmed! As Dawn Groves points out in her book *Meditation for Busy People*, "Chances are that an extra two minutes isn't going to upset anyone's schedule, but those same two minutes can make an enormous difference in how you handle yourself."

A word of warning: thinking about taking a moment to relax and center does not yield the same results as actually doing it. There is no promise of something for nothing. One must carry out the steps to experience the dance, no matter how simple they are.

Application Exercise

Once an hour today, take a moment to center.

1. Close your eyes (if possible).
2. Inhale, and hold the breath for a moment.
3. Exhale as you mentally count, "1."

Repeat steps 2 and 3 as you count up to 10. When you have finished, do a mental scan to notice what this exercise does for your body and being.

It is recommended that you do this at the same time each hour, perhaps on the hour. If, during the course of the day, there is an hour when this is not possible (or you forget), simply take the moment when you can (or when you remember).

At the end of each day, take a moment to write in your notebook any effects of your centering practice.

Remind Yourself

WHATEVER IS HAPPENING IN MY LIFE,
I TAKE A MOMENT TO CENTER AND RETURN TO MYSELF.

Week 16

Finding Peace in a Fast-Paced Environment

"Spirituality is not to be learned by flight from the world, by running away from things, or by turning solitary and going apart from the world. Rather, we must learn an inner solitude wherever or with whomsoever we may be."
—Meister Eckhart

PEACEFULNESS IS USUALLY ASSOCIATED WITH STILLNESS AND QUIET. So is it possible to find peace in a hectic workday? We think it is, and we have three suggestions.

1. *Prepare yourself.* When you know you are going to have a fast-paced day, make a plan before you hit the ground. Take a moment at the beginning of the day to clarify your goals and objectives. Specify the tasks you want to accomplish, stating why it is important for you to accomplish them, and what mental attitude, or state of mind, you would like to have as the day progresses. Make arrangements for small time-outs during the day for centering. This kind of strategizing is crucial. It is easier to make the decision for peace before the fast pace sets in than it is when you are already in the middle of it, unprepared and simply reacting to whatever comes next.

2. *Consider the fast pace as a form of meditation.* Many traditions of meditation involve being still. Others, though, involve movement, even fast movement. Tai Chi, martial arts, and the whirling dances of the Sufi tradition all focus on experiencing a calm center of peace within movement. Athletes—runners, swimmers, cyclists—recount experiences of "being in the zone" of relaxed awareness as a result of their intense movement. You can use these metaphors while you are in the middle of your fast-paced day. Simply use the

rhythm and swirl of the day around you to realize your own center of calm.

3. *Become an observer.* While you are busily moving through the day, take an occasional moment to mentally stand back and watch yourself performing your tasks. This mental attitude will help shift the stress you may be experiencing in the activity to a more detached and calm state in which you watch yourself progress through your work. It will also help you switch from reacting to things to welcoming them. Whether they are good or bad, satisfying or frustrating, you will be able to say, "I welcome you. You are part of a fast-paced environment, and you don't affect who I am."

Application Exercise

When you know you are going to have a fast-paced day, take a few moments before it starts to answer the following questions in your notebook:

1. What is my overall goal today?
2. What specific tasks do I wish to accomplish?
3. Why is it important to me to achieve this goal and accomplish these tasks?
4. What mental attitude or state of mind would I like to have today?
5. How and when will I take time to center?

Remind Yourself

Today I welcome everything that comes up.
I am a calm center in the midst of activity.

Week 17

Responding versus Reacting

"We don't see things as they are. We see them as we are."
—Anaïs Nin

REACTING IS AN AUTOMATIC AND EMOTION-BASED RESPONSE. Someone criticizes me, I am hurt, and I react with an angry retort. Responding, on the other hand, is based in thoughtful choices. Someone criticizes me, I am hurt, I pause for a moment and remember that nonviolence is one of my personal values, and I choose to acknowledge the hurt and seek reconciliation.

When we react emotionally to someone's comment or question, it is often because the person has touched an insecurity or past hurt in us. If you tell me that the job I have done is unsatisfactory, I might react in a hurt way, especially if I am afraid it is true, or if your words remind me of a similar remark from a teacher or boss in my past that made me feel inadequate.

If, however, I feel strong and confident about myself and my fundamental goodness, I might choose to respond in a variety of different ways. I might agree with you and decide to correct it. Or I might thank you for your observation, but state that I have a different view.

Here are two suggestions to help you respond rather than react. The first is to simply take a moment to stop. If a phone message or e-mail has upset you, avoid the temptation to immediately respond to the person. Take time to cool down and think about your response. If you are in face-to-face or telephone contact, pause, and take a deep, calming breath before answering.

Second, remember it is your interpretation that is upsetting you. If you find yourself reacting to someone's phone message or e-mail, ask yourself why you are having such a strong reaction. Give thought to other possible interpretations of their words. In conversations with people, repeat back what they have just said to make sure you heard them correctly and to give yourself time for a more thoughtful response. Then ask clarifying questions to focus your attention on their point of view, rather than your own reaction.

Shifting from reacting to responding is not easy, but it is important. It makes a world of difference in your ability to perform well in the workplace.

Application Exercise

If you find yourself being reactive today:

1. Gently ask yourself: Why am I upset about this? Each time you give an answer, gently ask yourself again, "Well, why am I upset about that?" After several questions and answers, you will start to discover the source of your reaction.
2. See the situation from the other person's point of view. Why did he or she make the comment or ask the question? Are there other possible ways to understand it?
3. Consider how you would choose to respond in a style that does not hurt you or the other person if you were totally free.
4. Take one example of a time today when you were reactive. Write down any insights you now have, using the preceding questions as a guideline.

Remind Yourself

I am the one who gives meaning to other people's words and actions.

Week 18
Water Off a Duck's Back

"What you think of me is none of my business."
—Terry Cole-Whittaker

HAVE YOU EVER THOUGHT ABOUT THE FACT THAT DUCKS LIVE AND move in water, and yet they do not get cold and wet? This is because their bodies secrete a special substance they spread over their feathers. This substance acts like a waterproof shield. It allows them to dive into the water for nourishment and emerge with water rolling off their backs while their bodies stay warm and dry.

What a clever mechanism, and what a great metaphor for the workplace! Think of the water as a metaphor for emotions, particularly negative emotions. Imagine the ability to go into an emotionally charged meeting, or to come into contact with stressful people, and have the negativity literally roll off, leaving you untouched.

It is possible to do this. Simply using the image of water rolling off a duck's back will help you. If you have to attend an intense meeting, remember the duck, and understand that you are entering an environment that has no power over you. Before you enter the situation, sit down and have a talk with yourself. Clarify your personal goals for the meeting. Focusing on these goals will help you avoid emotionality. Imagine the state of mind and body you would like to maintain during the meeting. Hold the image and phrase "water off a duck's back" in your mind. You will see it is possible to float above the sea of emotions and not be dragged down, drowned, or harmed in any way by them.

Whenever you find yourself in a negative situation—whether prepared or unprepared—keep the image of the duck in your mind. Make it real by reminding yourself: "Everything flows around me easily, like water. Emotions trickle over me, but nothing bogs me down. I have the ability to float above this."

These techniques will help you exercise your own personal power in any situation so that you, like the duck, can get what you need without being harmed.

Application Exercise

When you know you have to enter a difficult situation today, take a few minutes and do the following:

1. Center yourself, using the 10-breath routine described in Week 15.
2. Check in on your emotional state of well-being. Decide if there is anything you can do to strengthen or otherwise increase your well-being.
3. Focus on your personal goals. What do you want to achieve in the situation?
4. Relax your body, and imagine maintaining this relaxation during the meeting.
5. Imagine the state of mind you want to sustain during the meeting. Is it calm? Confident? Upbeat?
6. Now imagine a substance that will seal these feelings of well-being in your body and mind and repel anything you do not want to enter. Perhaps it is a large bubble or an orbit of light surrounding you.
7. Once again, center yourself using the 10-breath routine.

Take one example of a time today when you were in a difficult situation. Write how your responses changed after you did the preceding exercise.

Remind Yourself

I choose to let in only what is beneficial to me.
The rest is like water off a duck's back.

Week 19
Celebrating Your Accomplishments

"One never notices what has been done;
one can only see what remains to be done."
—Marie Curie

HAVE YOU EVER GOTTEN TO THE END OF A BUSY DAY AND WONdered if you accomplished anything? Life can get so hectic that you lose sight of the numerous tasks, actions, decisions, and thoughts accomplished in a day. Even though you engaged in a significant number of activities, a feverish pace can steal away your awareness of what you have accomplished as your attention dwells on what you have not.

There are two reasons why it is important to note what you have accomplished. First, humans thrive on encouragement. Observe how small children respond when they are praised for something they did. They beam, they blossom, and they want to do it again. In many work situations, other people may not be available to take note of our accomplishments, so we have to acknowledge and celebrate ourselves.

Second, noting our accomplishments boosts our self-esteem. If we constantly see only what has yet to be done, we will soon feel discouraged and overwhelmed by work. Never seeing the results of what we have attained may foster an underlying sense of failure. Taking time each day to recognize what we have accomplished produces satisfaction and pride in our work and faith in our ability to accomplish further tasks.

Taking time to reflect on what you have accomplished—today,

this month, or since starting your job—not only encourages you when things are going well, but sustains you when things are not. Having a solid sense of what you have done well in the past gives you the stamina to weather hard times, as well as belief in your ability to get through them.

Be aware that not every accomplishment has to do with checking a task off your "to do" list. Accomplishments also come in the form of lending emotional support to others, helping to resolve a conflict, asking a question at a meeting that brings clarification, taking the risk to put forth a new idea. Whenever you see that you have made a contribution to your own or the general effort, note it and congratulate yourself.

Application Exercise

Take a moment at the end of each day this week to reflect on and answer the following questions:

1. What have I accomplished today?
2. What have I accomplished this month?
3. What have I accomplished this year?
4. What have I accomplished since taking this job?

Your answer to the first question will change each day. For the other three questions, keep an open list that you can add on to each day, as you remember more and more things that you have accomplished.

Remind Yourself

I AM CONSTANTLY ACCOMPLISHING GOOD FOR MYSELF AND FOR OTHERS AROUND ME.

Week 20

Letting Go of Baggage

"The world comes to be what we believe it is."
—Gregory Bateson

IN COMMON PARLANCE, THE WORD "BAGGAGE" CAN REFER TO thoughts, ideas, and feelings from the past we continue to carry around. The past events that created our "baggage" are not relevant to the present. They block our view of what is actually going on today and keep us stuck in a limited or inaccurate view of what is happening.

Playing on the double meaning of "baggage," Dr. Jesse Jennings points out that we can lose our baggage when we "change planes." Although an unhappy thought for the frequent flyer, this metaphor can be powerful for those wishing to let go of emotional baggage. All it might take is a change of emotional planes.

Emotional planes act like actual aircraft, irrevocably heading toward a single destination. Staying in an emotional plane usually involves attachment to what happened in the past, what should have happened, why it didn't, and who was wrong. In other words, if we choose to remain in our emotional plane, we will continue to be burdened by our baggage of memories, impressions, and reactions. We will become tired, not because of what is happening right now, but because of what we are carrying with us. The only way to change our destination is to change planes.

I recently lost my baggage on a flight and was devastated because it contained business material I needed for a meeting the next day. I thought I would not be able to go on, that my progress would be hindered and things would simply not be the same.

I was right. Things were not the same. I was forced to be fully present at the meeting and approach the business from a fresh perspective. I was amazed at how well things went. I didn't even miss the freshly dry-cleaned suit I was sure would give me an advantage. Instead, I got to be myself in the moment and found that my presentation was more authentic as a result of having—literally and figuratively—no baggage.

I now try to apply this lesson when dealing with my clients. Before, when I first met a client, I tended to categorize him according to characteristics he shared with previous clients. In turn, I then had reactions to new clients that were not appropriate. When I notice this trend now, I mentally ask myself, "What if I had lost all that baggage on the flight? How would I approach this client differently?"

This week we invite you to examine your thoughts and feelings to see if they contain any outmoded baggage that you can let go of.

Application Exercise

Each day this week, choose a difficult situation (or person) in your life. In your notebook, make a list of what makes it (or him/her) difficult. For each point you have listed, answer the following questions:

1. Is this really true now?
2. Why do I think this?
3. What in my past experience has formed this belief?
4. Am I willing to let this go?
5. Is there another way of thinking about this?

Remind Yourself

MY LIFE CONSTANTLY PROVIDES OPPORTUNITIES TO THINK, FEEL, AND RESPOND IN NEW WAYS.

Week 21
Being at Choice

"Reality is really a process, undergoing constant transformation."
—Paulo Freire

AS CHILDREN, WE SEEM TO BE IN A WORLD THAT IS ALREADY SET. Everything is established—the characters, the circumstances, the rules. We have no choice; all is given.

As we mature, we gradually realize that we are able to exercise control over our lives. We come to understand that reality is not a static "given" state, but a dynamic process in constant change. We move from experiencing ourselves as stuck in a predestined life path to understanding that we are masters of our own destinies.

This can be difficult to remember, however, when we are in painful situations or in settings where others seem to be in power. At such times it is easy to feel victimized by circumstances rather than in control of them.

This is when the phrase "I am at choice" can be useful as a reminder that we are not limited by our circumstances. It helps us see that our life is bigger than the immediate, temporary situation. It encourages us to keep our mental muscles flexible, to think creatively and respond differently so that we do not get trapped by restricting events.

During times when you seem to have very little or no choice, a helpful exercise is to consider the choices you made which brought you to the present moment. As you cast your mind back to what got you here, you will see it was a series of choices. This exercise gives you a clear indication that the path of your future will also be one determined by your individual choices today.

Of course, it may not be as easy as immediately setting off in a completely new direction. But repeating the phrase "I am at choice" to yourself will increase your personal power to make small, moment-to-moment decisions that help you incrementally create the situation you want.

Application Exercise

1. List situations in which you experience yourself as being in control.
2. List situations in which you experience yourself as having minimal or no control. Reflect on the choices you made that brought you into these situations. Is there anything you can do differently in these situations to exercise your power of choice? Write down your thoughts.

Remind Yourself

IN EVERY MOMENT OF EVERY DAY,
I AM CHOOSING THE PATH OF MY LIFE.

Week 22
Quality Control

"We cannot do great things in this life.
We can only do small things with great love."
—Mother Teresa

QUALITY REFERS TO BOTH THE DEGREE OF EXCELLENCE WITH which we do a task and to the emotional condition or mental attitude we have when approaching a task. The quality of our tasks in the workplace creates the quality of our lives at work and, therefore, the quality of our total daily lives.

As Don Swartz says, "No one cares how much you know until they know how much you care." Certainly how much you care is reflected in the effort you put into the task at hand. Yet, in a busy workplace, there is the temptation to sacrifice quality for quantity.

Nonetheless, taking a quality approach to your tasks has several benefits. One is a boost in self-esteem and an increased sense of what is possible. When you do something to be proud of, you create positive energy for the next thing you need to do.

Other benefits include feelings of engagement, satisfaction, and accomplishment. When you put your whole being into your tasks, your level of self-expression feeds your body and your mind. Even if you do not complete the task, you can go home at the end of the day with the satisfaction that you gave it everything you could. Fundamentally, it is more satisfying to live with small, beautifully accomplished tasks than it is with a broad spectrum of mediocrity.

Naturally there are daily tasks we do not relish doing. When you look ahead to the tasks of the day, it is a good idea to carefully consider which are least pleasurable, and consider how you can bring more joy to them, perhaps by doing them at the time of day when you have your highest energy. This will help you be more "present" while doing them, which in turn will allow you to accomplish them with a higher level of excellence, giving you more pride and more joy in their accomplishment. In this way, you will greatly benefit from doing even the smallest and most unpleasant tasks as fully and completely as possible.

Application Exercise

Each day this week, list the tasks you need to accomplish. Identify the task that is least pleasurable for you. Consider how you can do it in a more joyful and personally satisfying way. What do you need to change about the way you do the task that would make it more pleasurable? Is there a different way for you to do it that will allow you to achieve a higher quality of performance? In your notebook, write down your ideas under the heading, "Ideas to Increase Joy and Improve Quality Today."

Remind Yourself

THE ATTITUDE AND QUALITY WITH WHICH I DO
A TASK IS MORE IMPORTANT THAN THE TASK ITSELF.

Week 23

Humanizing the Workplace

"My workday is so much more pleasant when I recognize that the people I work with are the most important part of my job, not the tasks I'm doing."
—Rob Morrison

HAS IT OCCURRED TO YOU THAT YOU SPEND A SUBSTANTIAL PART of your life at work? Sometimes we downplay the significance of this fact, acting as though our life is something that happens only after work hours. The truth is that your life is also happening right now, *at* work. So how can we feel more connected to our "real" selves in our jobs? Since we plan to spend a significant part of our day at work, how can we appreciate that investment of time rather than resent it?

Perhaps the answer lies in "humanizing" the workplace—seeing and internalizing your connection to human beings rather than to the job duties.

The first step is to become aware of how you interact with the people around you. This week, try to pay attention to what sort of conversations you have with people at work, in the elevator, on the phone, or elsewhere. Notice how your actions influence every person with whom you come into contact. Even though you may be working on a different project than another person is, think about how what you do could be connected to what they are doing. You might also want to give some thought to how your attitudes and actions affect others. For example, what happens to the other people in the room when you are late for a meeting? What happens to others in the room if you slouch and make no eye contact?

The next step is to explore the similarities between you and your co-workers. You can do what cultural anthropologists do when trying to understand a "foreign" culture—begin by looking at the most basic needs and activities all people have in common. Consider everyday activities such as answering the telephone, eating lunch, opening the mail. How do your co-workers do these things in the same way as you? How do they do them differently from you? Note what is the same and what is different.

As you increase your awareness of the humanity of your co-workers, the workplace not only becomes more pleasant, it becomes more productive. People like to help other people; functions tend to look out for themselves. Above all, you will start to see a community of people that nurtures and sustains you rather than a production system that drains and exhausts you.

Application Exercise

1. Select three co-workers and choose five activities that you all do at work (for example, eating lunch). Make notes about how each person carries out these activities. Notice where there are similarities and where there are differences between you and your co-workers. Then, ask yourself what conclusions you draw from this exercise. Use the following guide as you write in your notebook.

    Activity:
    How do I do it?
    How does person A do it?
    How does person B do it?
    How does person C do it?
    What is different and what is the same?

2. What conclusions do you draw from this exercise?

Remind Yourself

I AM SUSTAINED BY THE COMMUNITY
AND HUMANITY OF MY WORKPLACE.

Week 24
Like Attracts Like

"If you want a friend, be a friend."
—Ralph Waldo Emerson

THIS WEEK'S LESSON INTRODUCES A CONCEPT THAT CAN BE A challenge to the logical mind but can also be a very useful, practical tool for improving the quality of life. Simply stated, "like attracts like" means that whatever we do or think tends to attract more of the same, or similar, kinds of things.

One implication of this concept concerns how to expand the good that already exists in your life. Taking time to note the things, people, and events that you enjoy has the effect of inviting more such things into your experience. As you put your attention on these things, they will grow, expand, and prosper for you.

Another implication of the "like attracts like" concept concerns the things in our lives we do *not* like. We can use this idea as a gauge, noting what we do not like and looking within ourselves to assess in what way we may be contributing to the situation. Moreover, it is useful to note the things we do not like in order to consider how we might invite their opposites into our lives. In this way, we focus on how to improve things going forward.

A popular adage points out: "If you always think what you've always thought, you'll always get what you've always got." This saying encourages us to explore new ways to think about circumstances in our lives, especially the ones we do not like. For example, if you have a co-worker you dislike, try focusing on the good qualities he or she possesses. This experiment may result in you noticing and experiencing more good about and from this person.

"Like attracts like" helps us make positive changes in our circumstances. We all think about things we would like to do or have in our lives. This is a good starting place. But what will really set "like attracts like" into motion is action. Actually doing something toward your goal creates energy in your life that gives you momentum in that direction and also attracts other people and resources to help you.

So if there is something you have been wishing for, try taking a step toward it this week, and see if it doesn't also take a step toward you.

Application Exercise

1. In your notebook, list some things or people in your life you enjoy. What could you do to increase your enjoyment of them?
2. List some things in your life you do not like. For each of these, note the quality about it you do not like. Then, write down the opposite of that quality. (Example: my job—too dull—creative stimulation.) What could you do to have more of the "good" qualities in your life?
3. What is the number one new thing you have been wishing for? What is one action can you take this week toward having it?

Remind Yourself

As I move toward the things
I want in my life, they move toward me.

Week 25

Appreciating and Acknowledging Others

"The roots of all goodness lie in the soil of appreciation for goodness."
—The Dalai Lama

IN WEEK 19, WE ENCOURAGED OURSELVES BY APPLAUDING OUR accomplishments. We explored how tracking our own accomplishments uplifts us when things are going smoothly and when they are not. This week we look at the benefits of appreciating and acknowledging others.

A fundamental characteristic of all human beings is the desire to make a contribution that will benefit others. We are social creatures who want to feel like our efforts make a difference in the world. We thrive when other people notice and appreciate our contributions. When we feel as though we cannot make a contribution or that our contributions are not appreciated, we may begin to feel depressed or cynical.

Interestingly, one definition of "to appreciate" is "to rise in value." By appreciating a person, we offer him a valuable view of who he is to us, both in the present moment and in terms of his future contributions.

Naturally, some people may be easier for you to appreciate than others. There may be someone you work with who you think contributes nothing, or perhaps contributes something negative, such as anxiety. But even in this case there is the opportunity to say, "What does this person do for me, not just at the work place, but as a contribution to my overall life experience?"

You may find that appreciating and acknowledging others will have an ancillary benefit for you: Others will start to appreciate and acknowledge you more. If you withhold acknowledgment and appreciation, others may experience some discomfort around you and, therefore, may not give you acknowledgment. But as you appreciate and acknowledge people—even those you find difficult—you begin to radiate a certain inviting personal quality, making it easier for others to appreciate and acknowledge you.

Application Exercise

Identify five people who are central to your work life. Each day this week, select one and take a few moments to consider what you appreciate about him or her. Think about what he or she contributes to your day that makes your day "work." If possible, find a way to express your appreciation, and acknowledge each one of them. You can keep a written record noting:

Day 1: ____________ What s/he contributes to my workday:
(name)

Day 2: ____________ What s/he contributes to my workday:
(name)

Day 3: ____________ What s/he contributes to my workday:
(name)

Day 4: ____________ What s/he contributes to my workday:
(name)

Day 5: ____________ What s/he contributes to my workday:
(name)

Remind Yourself

I AM CONSTANTLY AWARE OF THINGS
TO APPRECIATE AND ACKNOWLEDGE IN OTHERS.

Week 26

Not Blaming

"Awakening from our sense of separateness is what we are called to do in all things."
—Ram Dass

ONE OF THE EASIEST WAYS TO CREATE AND MAINTAIN BARRIERS between yourself and other people is to blame them. Blaming fosters one or all of the following behaviors: defensiveness, hurt, attack, and counter-attack. Blame is a guaranteed way to instill an "us/them" mentality in the workplace.

But what happens when something goes wrong, when "stuff happens"? What should we do when an agreed-upon rule or system is violated? Does "not blaming" mean that everyone does whatever he or she likes? It certainly doesn't. It is important to look for and correct the cause of a mistake so that it does not happen again. The focus here is on how this is done.

For a workplace atmosphere to be safe, mature, and effective, each one of us must be accountable for the quality of communication. When a mistake happens, the way in which each person involved communicates will create the atmosphere that determines how the solution is achieved—whether with or without blame.

One way to uphold accountability and diminish blame is to objectively focus on the task, rather than slip into personal attacks. In other words, put the emphasis on dealing with observable data rather than interpretation, inference, and opinion.

Another way to reduce blaming is to understand your responsibility for the situation. Blame is a style of responding to the world in which I, the blamer, take no part of the responsibility for what happened. When I blame somebody, I am saying that I am completely without fault in the situation. So the first step to take when you are about to blame someone is to ask yourself how you helped create the situation or allowed it to occur.

Suppose, for example, that you need to get input from three people by Thursday in order to submit a report to your boss on Friday. Thursday comes and goes without their input, and on Friday your boss asks you for the report. Before you give the blameful response that your co-workers didn't give you the information you needed, consider first your own accountability. What was your role in not getting the information from them?

As each one of us soul-searches about our own responsibility instead of immediately reverting to blaming others, we will avoid the downward spiral of *who* is right, and rather begin to establish an upward spiral of *what* is right.

Application Exercise

This week whenever something goes wrong, answer the following questions about the situation in your notebook:

1. In what way did I contribute to this situation?
2. What can I do now to improve the situation?

Remind Yourself

I FOCUS ON MAKING THINGS BETTER IN THE FUTURE, RATHER THAN DWELLING ON WHAT WENT WRONG IN THE PAST.

Week 27
Living with Difficult People, Part I

"You have to learn to dance with a lot of different partners."
—Valerie Hamilton

IS THERE SOMEONE YOU LOATHE SEEING AT WORK? DO YOU EVER get the feeling that "everything would be all right if it just weren't for so-and-so?"

If so, you are creating a dangerous situation. When you believe someone is difficult (especially if you have evidence to back up your belief), your work experience around that person becomes charged with the expectation of difficulty. You might even experience feelings of dread before seeing such a person, and you might have feelings of anger and resentment after he or she has left. These responses will serve to expand your perception of unpleasantness so it becomes much greater than the unpleasantness you actually experience in his or her presence.

When you decide that it is another person who is causing your problems, you place yourself in a position of powerlessness, of being a victim. You effectively hand over to that person the power of deciding what quality of experience you will have.

For these reasons, it is important to take control and determine what the quality of your life will be whether or not this person is nearby.

The first step toward doing this is to increase your ability to see this person as a human being. Realize that somewhere in his life he is in situations in which he is not considered difficult. Open yourself up to the idea that this person could not only be loved, but is most likely being thought fondly of right now. Start to imagine the people who befriend and love this person.

Second, start to see what you have in common. Begin with something as simple as the fact that you may both wear glasses. When you are with the person, continue looking for things you have in common. This simple exercise will help shift focus away from your differences to your commonality, and will help you build bridges to that part of the person that is not difficult.

Third, think about what is good in this person. Write it down. Look for it when you are in his presence. Please note that this exercise is not intended to condone bad behavior or ignore transgressions such as breaking agreements. There are times when you must speak with the person about specific behaviors that have a negative impact on you or the work. What we suggest here is shifting your attention from negativity in others to their good. As we have pointed out before, what you put your attention on increases in your experience.

Application Exercise

Each day this week, think of a person you consider difficult. Spend a few moments each day writing down:

1. What do we have in common?
2. What is good about this person?

At the end of the week note the difference in your interactions with this person or your feelings about him.

Remind Yourself

There is good in everyone I meet.

Week 28
Living with Difficult People, Part II

"Objects in mirror are closer than they appear."
—Side Mirror, Many Cars

A HELPFUL TACTIC WHEN LIVING WITH A DIFFICULT PERSON IS TO analyze what exactly it is that you find difficult about him or her. Isolating the exact behaviors you find troublesome can help you understand that the whole person is not difficult, just certain things that he or she does. Perhaps it is not even the person at all but the specific activity you engage in together that affects your ability to respond in a positive way.

It may be helpful for you to begin exploring why certain behaviors "push your buttons." Is it because they remind you of someone from your past? For example, if what you find difficult is that the person barks orders at you, is this behavior reminiscent of a former teacher who intimidated you? This line of investigation can lead to the conclusion that you may be attributing more "difficulty" to the person than he or she actually warrants.

Once you have specified exactly which behaviors you do not like in the person, we suggest an exercise that has great potential to change the situation. It is based on the premise that we are all mirrors for each other. That is to say, other people reflect back to us qualities that we ourselves possess and behaviors in which we ourselves engage. For example, if someone in your life is bossy, you need to give serious consideration as to where in your life you are bossy.

Although this can be hard news to accept, it does have a very liberating aspect because, as we change for the better, we will also see more good in people around us. Using the above example, if you are able to stop being bossy, you will probably find that your "difficult person" will no longer be bossy (or he will no longer be in your life).

This week, spend some time thinking about the qualities and behaviors you see in other people—both those that seem good and those that seem negative. Consider what part of you is being reflected back, and if there is something in you that you want to change. You will know you are doing this exercise successfully as your life fills up with people you enjoy and admire.

Application Exercise

1. Think of someone you admire. List the things he or she does that you appreciate. Look over the list and consider how, in your life, you engage in these same behaviors.
2. Think of someone you consider difficult. List exactly what he or she does that you find difficult.
3. Look over the list. Ask yourself:
   Do these things remind me of something from my past?
   Do these things remind me of something I do?
   Am I willing to change any of my behavior patterns that are similar?

Remind Yourself

THE PEOPLE IN MY LIFE SHOW ME
HOW TO EXPRESS MORE GOOD IN MYSELF.

Week 29

When Good People Do Bad Things

"An angry voice is always about the speaker's own pain."
—Rev. Clay Johnson

AN UNDERLYING PREMISE OF THIS BOOK IS THAT HUMAN BEINGS are well intentioned. So, if people are innately good, why are there times they do not act that way?

As we have discussed in past weeks, it may be instructive for us to begin with an examination of ourselves. Can you recall a time when you did something seemingly out of character—something you thought was "bad" or "crazy"? When we do not act along the lines of our ideal behavior, we may later have a sense of shame or guilt and wonder, "Why did I do that?"

The answer may be that you were not reacting to the present situation, but to a past one. If you ever walked into work immediately after an argument at home, you know how the past can affect the present. It is important to understand that the long-ago, hidden past may be impacting your day-to-day dealings as well. A certain color, a particular phrase, or the way someone looks at you may spark a reaction from a past event. Those moments when you react in an unexpected, negative way can present a valuable opportunity for self-reflection. At those times, you can ask yourself, "Does the present situation remind me of something incomplete or painful from my past?"

This is helpful in three ways. First, when something goes wrong, it may be fruitful to look beyond the immediate issue for the source of discomfort. We usually focus on the problems at hand and do not stop to consider that they may be based on a larger picture.

Second, it helps us take these situations less personally. When other people overreact or seem to attack us, we can know there is a cause for their words and actions that has nothing to do with us. This eliminates our need to attack them back, be defensive, or berate ourselves for causing the incident.

Third, it helps us be less judgmental of others. When you are able to reflect on the reasons you have occasionally been off balance, you realize that this same force is at work in those around you.

Thinking about ourselves and others in this way gives meaning to the words of Victor Hugo: "The supreme happiness of life is the conviction of being loved for yourself, or more accurately, in spite of yourself."

Application Exercise

1. If you or someone you know does something hurtful or out of the ordinary this week, imagine that person as an innocent child, and ask yourself:
   What kind of past incident may have hurt this person and set up a pattern resulting in this action?
   What can I give this person in my mind—attention, love, words of kindness, or encouragement—to help in this past moment of pain?
2. Record any insights in your notebook.

Remind Yourself

I UNDERSTAND WHY GOOD PEOPLE, INCLUDING MYSELF, SOMETIMES ACT OUT OF CHARACTER.

Week 30

Being Compassionate versus Being a Doormat

"If circumstances are bad and you have to bear them, do not make them a part of yourself."
—Paramahansa Yogananda

EACH LESSON IN THIS BOOK IS AN INVITATION TO YOU. YOU ARE invited to see the greatest good possible in yourself and others in situations at work. You are called to rise to the challenge of exercising love and compassion even in the midst of negativity. But is there a point beyond which such an exercise is counterproductive?

In the quest to be more compassionate, you run the risk of confusing kindness with letting other people do what they want even when it has a negative impact on you. More dangerous still is the act of hiding your frustration and opinions behind a mask of "I'm a loving, compassionate person, and nothing can get to me."

So how do you know when enough is enough? What is the test for knowing when someone deserves understanding or deserves to be told he or she is being inappropriate? When is it okay to refuse a plea for help?

There are two things you can use as guides. One is your own set of life values and priorities. If your boss asks you to stay late on an evening when you promised to attend your child's school function, which is more important—responding to a request for assistance or breaking someone's trust?

The other readily available guide is your body. If someone is doing something that bothers you, but you are not sure if it bothers you enough to speak about it, bring your awareness to your body. You will quickly get a sense of how much tension the incident is causing you and whether it requires action on your part.

One word of caution: If you know you have a tendency toward being reactive, give yourself ample time to formulate your response. If you are experiencing tension in your body that indicates the situation does not feel right, it is appropriate to take time before giving your response. Perhaps rather than charging in to say something in the moment, you need to give yourself twenty-four hours. The point is to have the courage to know when something must be said and to find the right way to say it.

Application Exercise

Think of an incident in the past when something bothered you and you did not speak up, which left you with a sense of incompleteness about the situation. Answer these questions in your notebook:

1. What exactly bothered me in the situation?
2. What could I have said or done differently in order to change the situation?
3. Why was I not able to do that at the time?
4. If the situation were occurring now, how would I like to respond?
5. Is there anything I would need in order to respond this way?

Remind Yourself

I EXERCISE UNDERSTANDING AND
COMPASSION TOWARD MYSELF AS WELL AS OTHERS.
MY COMPASSION MAKES ME STRONGER, NOT WEAKER.

Week 31
Not Gossiping

"Our conversation should always be constructive, for to repeat gossip is to lengthen its life."
—Rev. Glen Hayden

GOSSIP IS A MAIN CONTRIBUTOR TO COMMUNICATION BREAKDOWN and an atmosphere of negativity and distrust. Gossip refers to speaking ill of others, to complaining about them to someone else. It is a dangerous use of time and energy because it not only creates feelings of distance between people, but it also has the potential to hurt others. It is not constructive in solving problems and allows the one gossiping to avoid taking responsibility for change.

The remedy? Whenever you have a complaint about someone, speak to that person directly. This may not seem like the easiest option, but in terms of well-being—both your own and that of your workplace—it is the healthiest. There is a saying that the easiest way out of a problem is usually the quickest way back into it. Direct communication, even if difficult, is the most logical solution because it is the most expedient way to improve the situation.

"Neutral" talk about other people—a general sharing of information—can also be considered gossip. Although this seems harmless, it can lead to misunderstanding. We all know what it is like to be in a "rumor mill," where the simplest of news gets transformed in the telling, often taking on a negative tinge. If you find yourself wanting to share information about someone else, first ask yourself these questions: Why am I doing this? How would I feel if someone were sharing this news about me? What is the benefit or value of this activity to all concerned?

Even in the seemingly compassionate act of expressing concern about another's misfortune, you might consider: "Are my words helping the situation, or am I just spreading my discomfort to others?"

This is not to suggest that you must react self-righteously if you are in a situation with people who are speaking about others. The question for you is simply, "Am I going to participate?"

To get a sense of the benefits of not indulging in gossip, consider: What if you had a reputation in your workplace as someone who only had positive words to say about other people? What if you were known in your workplace as someone who addressed issues directly with the person involved? What if everyone knew that if they shared something personal with you, it would go no further? It is easy to see that you would become known as a person who is trustworthy and safe—one with whom people can relax and feel totally at ease.

Application Exercise

Whenever you find yourself speaking to someone about someone else this week, gently ask yourself the following questions and answer them in your notebook:

1. Why am I speaking about him or her? What is my true motive?
2. Are my words helping to create harmony in myself, in others, and in my world?
3. Would I appreciate it if someone were speaking about me like this?
4. What is stopping me from speaking *to* this person rather than *about* this person?
5. Is there anything else I should be doing rather than speaking about this person?

Remind Yourself

MY WORDS CREATE HARMONY IN MY WORLD.
I AM A TRUSTWORTHY PERSON.

Week 32
Suspending Judgment

"When we lose our interest in other people's character flaws, we become flawless."
—Rev. Nancy Zala

THIS WEEK WE EXAMINE HOW AND WHEN WE JUDGE OTHERS. Suspending judgment does not mean you give up discernment, ethical reasoning, expressing preferences, or honestly acknowledging your reactions to things. Rather, it should encourage you to become aware when you are sitting in judgment of others—passing judgment on their value and character—and mentally demeaning them. Anytime you find yourself thinking that you are better than someone else, you have judged them. And anytime you find yourself thinking that someone is better than you, you have judged yourself.

What we are advocating instead of an attitude of judgment is the recognition that we are all doing the best we can and a receptivity to understanding why others act the way they do.

There are two good reasons to adopt this attitude. First, it is healthy. Notice the physiological state you assume when you judge someone else; observe where in your body your muscles tighten. When you are accepting others, your body is in a healthy state of open relaxation. This point is driven home by the question: "Would you rather be right or happy?"

Second, the familiar Bible quote, "Judge not that ye be not judged," encapsulates what happens when we judge others; we feel judged by them. Have you ever spoken at a meeting and felt embarrassed because you knew others were mentally criticizing you? If so, you probably have a tendency to criticize others in that situation. As you reduce your judgment of other people, you will find a corresponding decrease in your feelings of being judged by them.

A final and important consideration is that we usually judge people when we are feeling "less than" or inferior. One of the most instructive things you can do when you find yourself judging others is to ask yourself the question: What are these thoughts pointing to in my life that I need to pay attention to or take care of?

Application Exercise

Anytime this week you notice yourself sitting in judgment toward another person:

1. Imagine that you are that person, and explain your actions from his or her point of view.
2. Consider what exactly it is about this situation that bothers you. Does this indicate some aspect of your own character or behavior that you want to change?
3. Write your discoveries and thoughts in your notebook.

Remind Yourself

I AM OPEN TO UNDERSTANDING OTHER PEOPLE'S WORDS AND ACTIONS FROM THEIR POINT OF VIEW.

Week 33
Accepting Other People's Mistakes

"He who smiles rather than rages is always the stronger."
—Japanese Wisdom

IN WEEK 5, WE ENCOURAGED YOU TO EXERCISE MORE COMPASSION and understanding toward yourself when you make a mistake. We advocated seeing your own mistakes as necessary for growth. This week we extend that compassion and understanding to others, recognizing that other people are also in a developmental process, and that their mistakes are also necessary—perhaps even unavoidable—for their growth.

Accepting that other people will make mistakes as a natural part of doing their jobs does not preclude you from speaking to them about their mistakes. The question becomes, rather, *how* you speak to them. We recommend speaking in a way that is gracious and understanding, one that is based on the viewpoint that there is a justifiable reason for the person's mistake. This empathetic approach includes the possibility that, given the same circumstances as this person, you could have made the same mistake.

There are two wonderful benefits of being understanding and gracious about other people's mistakes. First, it encourages them to continue working with you. Think about your own experience of people who have been impatient with your mistakes. You can appreciate how quickly this approach can make a person feel disempowered and discouraged.

Second, it is just about guaranteed there will come a time when you will make a mistake that impacts other people. If you have been intolerant and judgmental of others' mistakes, they will relish the opportunity to pounce on you. If you have been gracious with them, they will be gracious with you.

The word *gracious* comes from *grace*, which in religious terms refers to receiving love for no reason. There is nothing you can do to deserve it; it is a gift with no strings attached. Being gracious with others emulates that quality. They do not have to do anything to deserve the high esteem you freely hold for them. And when they make mistakes, you give them the benefit of the doubt without requiring explanation or retribution.

Application Exercise

1. Think about a time when you made a mistake and someone spoke to you about it in an intolerant, judgmental way. Write about it in your notebook. How did you feel? What are the specific things he or she said and did that you want to be sure not to do when addressing others' mistakes?
2. Think about a time when you made a mistake, and someone spoke to you about it in a gracious, understanding, and empathetic way. Write about it in your notebook. How did you feel? What are the specific things he or she said and did that you want to be sure to do when addressing others' mistakes?
3. If someone makes a mistake that impacts you, consider: What are the things this person has done well in the past? What are the possible reasons that this mistake was made? Is there any way you could have made the same mistake?

Remind Yourself

I AM A GRACIOUS, UNDERSTANDING, AND ACCEPTING PERSON.

Week 34

Telling the Truth Kindly

"If it's very painful for you to criticize your friends,
you're safe in doing it. But if you take the slightest pleasure in it—
that's the time to hold your tongue."
—Alice Duer Miller

CRITICISM CAN BE DEVASTATING, ESPECIALLY IF THE MESSAGE comes as a complete surprise to the recipient. It can be even more damaging when the criticism is delivered with the axe-like attitude of, "Well, I am just telling the truth."

It is this association of hurt with truth-telling that can stop us from saying things that need to be said. We may shy away from saying difficult things because we are afraid we will hurt the person. Ironically, by not speaking, we actually increase the potential for further harm.

So the challenge becomes one of how to speak up when necessary, in such a way that the other person is not damaged or hurt or thinks any less of himself; how to be honest with someone in a way that is not blameful or judgmental, but is empowering.

The starting point is to approach the situation compassionately, realizing that you are dealing with a real person with real feelings and to put yourself into that person's shoes upon receiving this news.

The second step is to consider your motive for delivering this message. Alice Duer Miller's quote above is helpful in determining whether you have any self-righteous intentions or if you are truly doing this for the benefit of the person involved. A good question to ask yourself is: How valuable is this message to the well-being of the person?

There are several techniques advocated in management courses that are helpful in telling the truth kindly. These include asking the person's permission to speak, focusing on the issue rather than the personality, and using "I" statements instead of "you" statements when possible.

But the most important thing is to be vigilant in assessing your own motives. This will ensure that you are indeed concerned with bringing about greater good for the person or people involved. If this is truly your intention, it will be easier to deliver your message so that the person concerned experiences the respect, love, and support intended for him.

Application Exercise

1. Reflect on times when people have told you the truth. These may have been hurtful to you or they may have been empowering. As you reflect on these memories, make two lists in your notebook with these headings: "Things To Avoid Doing When Telling The Truth" and "Things To Do When Telling The Truth."
2. If there is somebody to whom you need to speak the truth, answer these questions:
   What is the issue here?
   What am I afraid of saying? Why?
   What do I want to say?
   Why am I saying this?
   Why do I think this is necessary?
   How will this help the person?
   What are some different ways I can say this?
   How will I communicate my respect, love, and support?
   How will this increase the awareness or experience of good?

Remind Yourself

I TELL THE TRUTH IN SUCH A WAY THAT OTHERS EXPAND THEIR AWARENESS AND EXPERIENCE OF GOOD IN THEIR LIVES.

Week 35
Why Complain?

"It is a poor workman who blames his tools."
—Arabic Proverb

HAVE YOU EVER KNOWN PEOPLE WHO COMPLAIN ABOUT THE SAME thing for long periods of time? At first you may have been sympathetic to their problems, but over time you probably wondered why they haven't done anything to remedy the situation. Eventually their complaints become boring and annoying.

This is the problem with complaining—it keeps us stuck. Sometimes people get stuck in the past—dwelling on things already handled, changed, or out of their control. This futile exercise destroys a sense of community by emphasizing and sustaining negativity.

Complaining about things currently happening is equally counterproductive. Since it is a substitute for action, it keeps us stuck where we are. It also allows us to cast ourselves in the disempowering role of the victim—one who has no control.

The Serenity Prayer is relevant here, in which one asks for "the strength to accept the things I cannot change, the courage to change the things I can, and the wisdom to know the difference." For those things that are past and beyond control, silence may be a better option than complaining.

But for those things that are within our control, action is more effective than complaining. We are not suggesting that you remain silent if something negative is currently happening. Instead, we encourage you to use your words and actions to solve the problem rather than to complain about it.

The positive thing about complaining is that it raises a red flag that something is wrong. The negative thing is that it extends, rather than solves, the problem.

The next time you find yourself on the verge of complaining about something, stop and ask yourself two questions: "Will my words help the situation?" and "What can I do to remedy the situation?"

Application Exercise

For any situation you find yourself complaining about this week, answer the following questions in your notebook:

1. What is the situation?
2. What exactly is bothering me about this situation?
3. What do I want in this situation?
4. What is my solution for this situation?
5. What do I need to do in order to achieve that solution?

Remind Yourself

I HAVE ALL THE RESOURCES I NEED
TO REMEDY SITUATIONS I DO NOT LIKE.

Week 36

Accepting Support

"We cannot live for ourselves alone. Our lives are connected by a thousand invisible threads, and along these sympathetic fibers, our actions run as causes and return to us as results."
—Herman Melville

IN TODAY'S WORKPLACE, IT IS EASY TO BECOME OVERWHELMED with work. When we have more work than we can handle, we can feel isolated and victimized by the thought of "Why am I the only one working so hard?"

The remedy is to ask for help, but many of us find this difficult. There are a variety of reasons for this, including: a fear of appearing weak or looking incompetent; a reluctance to bother or be indebted to others; and a belief that it is easier to do it yourself or that someone else will not do it as well as you. Perhaps you have had a bad experience with people who asked for help too much, yet were not pulling their own weight. This week, we explore how to balance asking for help, receiving help, offering help, and giving help.

The difficulty of giving and receiving help is heightened in jobs where there is minimal contact with other people. In such jobs, one may start to think that there is no connection with others and, therefore, no one to ask for or to offer help to. But even here, a few moments of thought reveal how interdependent we really are and how much each individual job intertwines with others.

If you need to increase your ability to either give or receive support, you can begin with nonessential things or during non-critical times. It is much easier to ask for help with something in which you do not have a great deal invested than it is to turn over to someone else something that is very important to you. Similarly, it is easier to approach someone with a general offer of help when things are going smoothly rather than when they are in a crisis mode and perhaps not able to take the time to accept your offer.

Another important aspect of both accepting and offering support is ensuring that the communication of the request or offer is complete. When someone offers help, graciously acknowledge that you could use some assistance, and then find out exactly what they are offering, both in terms of time and in terms of skill. Are they simply offering a well-meaning indication of support or is there a specific way the person wants to help you? On the flip side, it is good to be clear about your own intention and commitment to follow through when you offer help.

As each of us improves our ability to ask, receive, offer, and give help, the workplace environment transforms from one of competition, isolation, and stress to one of collaboration, interdependence, and balance.

Application Exercise

1. At the end of each day this week, note instances of when you asked for, received, offered, and gave support. Record your observations under these four headings: Asked for support; Received support; Offered support; Gave support.
2. As you look over your list each day, answer these questions:
   What were your thoughts and feelings in each case?
   Which of the four categories is easiest for you?
   Which do you do the most?
   Which would you like to do more often?
   What are specific steps you can take to do this?

Remind Yourself

As I give and receive support,
the workplace becomes a more pleasant place to be.

Week 37
Encouraging Yourself

"Negative attitudes—especially about yourself—
are like excess baggage. They weigh you down unnecessarily
and interfere with your freedom of movement."
—Sarah Dening

HAVING JUST LEARNED TO DO THE BACKSTROKE, SIX-YEAR-OLD Ariana Kaiser decided to swim on her back across the rather substantial width of the pool. As she inched along, she said to herself, "Come on, Ari. You can do it. Keep going. You're almost there." When she accidentally stroked water over her face, she kept on, saying, "It's okay. You're doing great. Keep going." She beamed with pride when she arrived at the far side of the pool.

Witnessing this event gave rise to the thought: What do I do to encourage myself in new and challenging circumstances? Do I give myself credit for what I attempt and what I accomplish, or do I put myself down for feeling awkward and being inadequate?

As we explored in Week 10, how we talk to ourselves has a big impact on our experience of life. This is particularly crucial to remember in new or challenging situations. Being on unfamiliar terrain adds to a sense of vulnerability. In difficult situations, where we feel we are being closely scrutinized or even under attack, there seems to be no lack of people pointing out our mistakes. At these times, it is especially important to be our own champion.

One helpful guideline for self-encouragement is to consider how you would speak to a child who is learning a new skill or to an adult friend struggling through a difficulty. Would you express impatience and point out their weaknesses, or would you compassionately acknowledge the troublesome nature of the situation and applaud them for their accomplishments? We could bring the same sort of leniency and appreciation to ourselves as we would provide for others.

You can also encourage yourself in deed as well as in thought. Whatever you would do to express appreciation to someone else for a job well done, you can do for yourself, whether it is a note of thanks and congratulations, a special lunch, or a bouquet of flowers. This has the effect of boosting your morale, and it also reminds you that, among the many facets that form "you," there is a part that holds the highest view of you at all times. This part of you is not discouraged or affected by temporary situations and is always available as a source of strength.

Application Exercise

1. For this week's exercise, think of a situation that is challenging for you.
2. As you go through the day, keep track of the things you tell yourself about the situation. Note the inner messages that are encouraging and supportive, and the things that are discouraging and critical. Mentally compare these things and consider which you prefer and would like to increase.
3. Write three things you can say to encourage yourself in this situation.
4. Sometime this week, do something special to honor your achievements. This could be in the form of a congratulatory letter, a certificate of appreciation, a bouquet of flowers, a special lunch, a gift, or other treat.

Remind Yourself

I AM ALWAYS DOING THE BEST I CAN IN ANY SITUATION.

Week 38
Engaging Your Creativity

"When you think you've exhausted all possibilities, remember: you haven't."
—Thomas Edison

MANY PEOPLE DO NOT CONSIDER THEMSELVES CREATIVE. WHAT A misconception! To be human is to be creative. Each time we speak, we are being creative. Every moment of the day, you express your unique creativity in everything you do. It may appear that some people are more creative than others. In reality, we are all creative. It is simply a matter of how aware we are of our creativity and how much we use it.

One example of creativity in the workplace occurs when we are presented with new problems for which new solutions are needed. And in times of rapid change, these opportunities are becoming more frequent.

But you do not have to be faced with something new and unknown to become creative. You can practice creativity on a regular basis in ordinary situations. Think of it like any skill you develop, such as playing the piano or bowling. The more you practice and exercise your creativity, the more creative you will become. Practicing your creativity on a daily basis in small matters can help prepare you for those critical times when you will need to be even more creative.

Exercising your creativity can help you get "unstuck" in those areas where you feel stagnant. If there is some area of your life that feels stale—either at work or at home—it is probably because you have fallen into a repetitive routine of thinking about it and doing it.

A good way to begin is with a tedious or repetitive task. Finding new ways to do your tasks will make them more interesting. When you have been doing the same thing in the same way for a long time, the chore becomes static and monotonous. You may become rigid in your thinking, believing that there is only one way it can be done. Before you get into that kind of rut, consider doing things differently so that you can stay fresh. As you become used to thinking of alternative ways to do things, you become more vital and creatively alive in the workplace.

Look at what you are doing this week and ask yourself, "How can I do this in a different way? How can I do this in a way that would feel better? What can I do to my work environment to make it stimulate my creativity?"

Application Exercise

Each day this week, do something differently. (For example, choose a different way to go to work, write down your morning routine and do it backwards, change your lunch routine.) For each day, make a note of any thoughts or feelings the act generated in you by recording: (1) what you did differently; (2) the thoughts and feelings that arose.

Remind Yourself

As I choose to use my creativity,
my life is more interesting and rewarding.

Week 39

Lighten Up!

"You will do foolish things. But do them with enthusiasm!"
—Colette

HUMORIST STEVE BERMAN CITES RESEARCH FINDING THAT CHILdren laugh an average of 100 times a day, whereas adults laugh an average of 14 times a day. What happens to us as we grow up? At what point do we lose the delight in ourselves and the world around us?

One thing that happens is we start to take ourselves quite seriously, becoming overly concerned about what people think of us. We want to be perceived as intelligent and competent. Frivolity does not seem to fit this picture. Looking foolish, even in our own eyes, becomes forbidden.

This is a shame, for in giving up our ability to laugh at ourselves, we also become timid about stepping forward and being seen. How many people pass up opportunities to speak in public, to give an opinion, or even to ask a question at a meeting for fear of looking foolish?

As we release unrealistic and unhealthy standards of perfection for ourselves, we become more able to embrace ourselves as we truly are—with all of our human glory and foibles. This allows us to forgive ourselves for past mistakes, to truly accept and love ourselves. As we let go of the need to defend ourselves from "looking bad," we loosen up and become relaxed and flexible. Not only are we able to take more risks—like speaking up when needed—but we begin to actually enjoy being ourselves.

Becoming light-hearted about yourself is a great gift for others around you in two ways. First, from your own experience with overly sensitive people, you can relate to that cautious "walking on eggshells" feeling. As you lighten up, people around you can relax the need to guard their speech and action for your sake. Second, your willingness to laugh at yourself allows others room to be less than perfect. They feel secure and comfortable in the fact that they can be themselves with you, and they trust that if they do something foolish, you will still accept them.

The word *enlighten* can be understood in two ways—to become wiser and to take on a lighter or less serious attitude. This week we encourage you to lighten up and see what wisdom comes to you as a result.

Application Exercise

1. Swap "most embarrassing moment" stories with others in the workplace. As you hear their stories, you may notice that, far from losing any respect for them, your fondness and empathy for them increases. (Remember this the next time you do something embarrassing.)
2. Think about the silliest thing you have done at your current job. Compare how you felt about it at the time with how you feel about it now.
3. Think of someone you like and imagine that he or she had done the embarrassing and silly things that you did. How would you feel about him or her?
4. Record your observations and insights in your notebook.

Remind Yourself

As I lighten up my attitude toward myself,
I increase enjoyment for myself and for others.

Week 40
Acknowledging Your Strengths

"One of the worst of my many faults is that I'm too critical of myself."
—Ashleigh Brilliant

THIS BOOK IS ABOUT EXPANDING YOUR ABILITY TO PERCEIVE AND experience good, in both the people and circumstances around you as well as in yourself. Some might even argue that seeing good within yourself is a necessary starting point—that your sense of self-esteem determines how you perceive others.

Unfortunately, it is possible for one's sense of self-esteem to get worn down in the workplace. This can happen where there is an atmosphere of blame and fear or where there is a rigid hierarchy of job status and power. Self-esteem can also suffer if your job requires you to use your less well-developed skills so that doing your job becomes a struggle for you. Even the best of jobs does not use all of our strengths, all of our talents. The more we creatively express ourselves through our talents, the better we feel.

This week we encourage you to take a step back from your job and remove yourself from the limitation of identifying yourself with it. Instead, look at yourself as a total expression of creativity that includes, but is more than, your job. As you begin to reflect on your strengths and talents, some will be more obvious (for example, math or writing skills), whereas others will be more subtle (such as putting others at ease).

Thinking about your strengths and talents has two benefits. First, it increases appreciation for what you currently bring to your job. This is an important idea to hold foremost in your mind when people try to belittle you or events at work do not unfold as you would like. Second, it expands your view of what you have to offer over and beyond your current job, pointing the way to a more fulfilling experience of expressing who you truly are.

Each one of us is a multi-talented, creative, and unique expression of life. We invite you to put aside any sense of false humility—including the impossible idea that you have little or nothing to offer—and enjoy exploring your strengths and talents.

Application Exercise

1. Make two lists in your notebook: "Character/Personality Strengths" and "Special Skills and Talents." After listing all the strengths and talents you can think of, add to the lists by asking friends, family, and co-workers what they think are your strengths, skills, and talents.
2. As you look at your lists, consider which of these are being used in your current job?
3. Next, consider what did you like to do—or were good at doing—as a child? Which of these activities would you be interested in revisiting?
4. Record any insights in your notebook.

Remind Yourself

I HAVE MANY STRENGTHS, SKILLS,
AND TALENTS TO OFFER THE WORLD.

Week 41
Other Ways to Do Things

"If all you have is a hammer,
then all your problems will be seen as nails."
—Abraham Maslow

MANY OF US GREW UP WITH THE IDEA THAT FOR EVERY PROBLEM there is a right answer and a wrong answer—a view emphasized in traditional education. As adults, we may be surprised to learn there can be more than one right answer for any problem. In fact, it can be fun and creatively stimulating to occasionally ask yourself, "What is the other right answer to this question?"

Similarly, we can fall into the habit of thinking that our way of doing a thing is the only way to do it, or certainly the best way. We may even look with mystification or disdain at our colleagues who go about their work in a different, seemingly less efficient manner.

If you have ever taken a personality test, you may be aware that people access, process, and apply information in different ways. Some of us prefer to start with the bottom line and then move into the details; others prefer to begin with a careful description of the details leading up to the conclusion. Those of us who are extraverts tend to think out loud, developing an answer through talking about it. Those of us who are introverts may first take time to discover the answer internally before speaking about it. Some of us take in information best when reading it, others by hearing it. These are just a few of the many differences between us that impact how we do our work.

Remembering that people around you have different work

styles has three benefits. First, it helps remove judgment. For example, just because someone is quieter (or more talkative) than I am has nothing to do with intelligence, confidence level, or degree of sanity. It is simply a different yet valid way of being. This nonjudgmental attitude allows us to take the next step of sitting down with work colleagues and discussing work style preferences. This results in greater understanding, tolerance, and respect for each other, as well as the building of mutual support.

Second, when we realize that not everyone in the workplace learns and processes information in the same way, we can consider how to make information and work interactions accessible to everyone. Perhaps sending a message by e-mail *and* voice mail is the more efficient method of communicating to a group, especially if it ensures that more people will receive and understand the information.

Third, opening ourselves up to different ways of doing things allows us to remain flexible in our thinking, which leads to a richer life experience with more positive results in our work.

Knowing that there are many ways to do something, look around you this week and begin to explore how your work style is the same as or different from your colleagues—not better or worse, just different.

Application Exercise

This week's exercise reminds you that there are different, valid ways of being and working. Here are five questions to answer about yourself in your notebook:

1. If faced with a problem, I prefer to solve it by: (a) discussing it with others; or (b) thinking it over by myself.
2. When concentrating on a work task, I prefer: (a) to have quiet; or (b) to work with music or some other background sound.
3. When people describe situations, I prefer they: (a) give me the conclusion first, and then add details; or (b) build the case using details before giving me the conclusion.

4. I prefer to have explanations: (a) in writing; or (b) explained orally.
5. When working with a group, I tend to focus on: (a) whether we are accomplishing our goal; or (b) the manner in which we are relating to each other as we work together.

Discuss the questions above with two (or more) colleagues. As you review your answers and those of your colleagues, make notes of things to remember when working together.

Remind Yourself

There are many right ways to do anything.

Week 42

Celebrating Other People's Success and Good Fortune

"I will not meanly decline the immensity of good, because I have heard that it has come to others in another shape."
—Ralph Waldo Emerson

In Weeks 11 and 12, we explored the role of gratitude in creating the experience of more good in our lives. By training ourselves to notice and appreciate the good that already exists, we extend our ability to perceive even more good.

Furthermore, everything we say and do sends a message to our entire being. By being grateful for something, we essentially program ourselves to receive more of it. Expressing gratitude is like declaring, "Yes! I like that and I want more." Both of these ideas are contained in Mary Baker Eddy's statement that if we are "really grateful for the good already received...we shall avail ourselves of the blessings we have, and thus be fitted to receive more."

This holds true not only for the good we see in our own lives, but also for the good we see in other people's lives. When you see others' successes and you are happy for them, you are telling yourself, "I approve of success," and your being will respond by creating success in your own experience.

Conversely, when you see others' successes and you are unable to celebrate them, you tell yourself, "I don't approve of success."

We all know we get better at anything when we practice. If you practice being dissatisfied when others are successful, you increase your capacity to feel that way about your own success. This distances you from the type of feeling associated with success. That feeling is important because it creates the environment in which success is welcome.

Imagine trying to give a gift to someone who is not willing to receive it, or who is so disappointed that someone else has a gift that he or she doesn't even notice you are offering your gift. Perhaps this is how the world works. Perhaps it is hard for us to receive a promotion or a raise at work when our mental environment has so much animosity toward the idea of success that we are not welcome recipients.

The next time you see someone experience good, you can practice celebrating success, both within the privacy of your own thoughts and by congratulating the person. The more you do this, the more you increase your own capacity for success in your life.

Application Exercise

1. In your notebook list five people in your life who have recently experienced success (large or small). Write their names and what they did or received.
2. This week, write a congratulatory note to each person, acknowledging his or her accomplishments or good fortune.

Remind Yourself

By celebrating others' good,
I invite good into my own experience.

Week 43
Taking Risks

"You gain strength, experience, and confidence by every experience where you really stop to look fear in the face. You must do the thing you cannot."
—Eleanor Roosevelt

THROUGHOUT THIS BOOK, WE HAVE BEEN WORKING TO EXPAND the good in our lives by addressing both our thoughts and our actions. This week we use both mental and physical tools to prepare for action in taking a risk.

By "taking a risk," we are not talking about risks that are unsafe, harmful to you or others, or haven't been well thought out. We are not advocating taking a risk simply for risk's sake.

What we are considering are those areas in your life where you feel stifled by your own fear of action. We are talking about those things you have wanted to do, have, or be, but have been restricted from by your concerns about the outcome. We are calling to mind things you have been thinking about and yearning for. Perhaps it is asking for a raise, applying for a new position, or confronting a colleague. Taking this kind of risk—putting yourself in a situation where you may feel fearful—is a natural evolution in your growth.

These kinds of risks that are necessary for our growth bring to mind the words of writer Erica Jong: "If you don't risk anything, you risk even more"; and of opera singer Beverly Sills: "You may be disappointed if you fail, but you are doomed if you don't try."

So how can you support yourself in standing powerfully and taking the risk? Willpower will have only a limited effect. It may get you into the situation, but it will not prepare you to handle it in an elegant or confident way. To prepare yourself, you need to engage your imagination in a rehearsal process.

The first step is to identify what you want to do. At this point, you may notice an uncomfortable feeling of resistance in both mind and body. This is natural, and it will diminish over time as you get used to the idea of doing "the thing you cannot."

The next step is to imagine yourself in the situation. If it is a situation involving speaking, write out the words you need to say. Now practice saying them. Even if you feel awkward or silly, you have already taken a big step by physically speaking this difficult thing out loud as opposed to being defeated by the mere thought of how nervous you would be saying it.

As you continue in your rehearsal process, practicing your "script" over hours, days, or even weeks, you will transform. Your initial feelings of silliness, nervousness, or irritation will fall away. Repeating the words will imbue them with meaning, conviction, and clarity. Each time you rehearse, you will come closer to being the person who can actually say these words. You will move from artificiality to authenticity.

At some point, you will feel a compelling urge to say the words to the person, and then you will know it is time to step forward. Of course, the scene may not work out exactly as you scripted it in your mind. Nevertheless, your preparation will allow you to act and respond in a powerful way.

Application Exercise

1. Bring to mind something you have wanted to do—something that is for your own benefit, is harmful to no one, and seems risky to you.
2. In your notebook, describe the situation.
3. Then answer the following questions:
   How do you feel—in mind and body—when you think of doing this?

What is the worst thing that can happen if you do this?
What is the best thing?

4. Take a few moments to close your eyes, breathe, and relax your body. Pay particular attention to relaxing and opening your chest area.
5. Imagine yourself in the situation. Now, write the words you need to say or the action you need to take.
6. Practice saying the words out loud, or imagine doing the action. Note the feelings that come up as you practice.

You will know you have rehearsed enough when you start to feel a compelling urge to actually say these words to the person you need to talk to, or to complete the task. After you have done so, you can record your thoughts about this process.

REMIND YOURSELF

I AM WILLING TO PREPARE MYSELF
AND EXPAND MY CAPACITY FOR TAKING RISKS.

Week 44
The High View

"Given the choice, choose the kind thought."
—Maureen McNamara

THIS WEEK WE INVITE YOU TO THINK ABOUT THE HIGH VIEW IN ALL situations, particularly difficult ones. The high view does not mean looking down on others or denying the reality of a situation. The high view simply refers to seeing the broader perspective—the bigger picture. A good illustration is provided by Eric Butterworth in his book *Spiritual Economics*. Butterworth describes a British couple's first visit to New York City. They arrived with some trepidation, expecting a crime-ridden city. The first thing their host did was to take them to the top of a tall building from which they could view the whole city. This gave them a positive initial impression, which extended throughout their visit. As they later saw the sights from ground level, the memory of the view from the top remained. After a wonderful week, they left New York, calling it the "loveliest, friendliest, and finest place we have been." Such is the power of the initial high view.

The high view is an important antidote to our mental tendency to be drawn into what is dramatic, as opposed to what may be valuable, in a situation. Notice what happens if you are involved in a deep conversation in a restaurant, and someone nearby starts to argue. Does your focus stay on the important conversation at hand or drift toward the passionate words being spoken? Notice what happens among friends when scandalous gossip arises. Do they gravitate toward the valuable or toward the dramatic?

The high view encourages us to take in as much of the situation as possible—not just a limited, small portion of it. This helps us be more fully present in a situation. Far from a way of escaping a situation, the high view invites us to lean into its full reality.

Reminding ourselves to take the high view has three benefits. First, we can enjoy new and different responses to situations beyond the familiar, well-traveled, often negative ones. Second, we lessen our judgmental attitudes toward ourselves and others. And third, we get to experience a light-hearted sense of liberation from the trap of petty struggles and antagonisms. Enjoy!

Application Exercise

1. This week, if you find yourself in a difficult, challenging, or uncomfortable situation, simply ask yourself: What is the highest thought I can think about this situation?
2. If you find yourself being judgmental of someone else, pause and ask yourself: What is the highest thought I can think about him/her?
3. If you find yourself feeling badly about yourself, gently ask yourself (as though addressing a cherished friend): What is the highest thought I can think about myself right now?
4. Write down your answers in your notebook.

Remind Yourself

I STAY IN TOUCH WITH MY OWN GOODNESS,
NO MATTER WHAT IS HAPPENING.

Week 45

Starting Again

"You may have a fresh start any moment you choose, for this thing we call 'failure' is not the falling down, but the staying down."
—Mary Pickford

THERE IS A SUBTLE, WIDESPREAD NOTION THAT IF THINGS GET going in the wrong direction, they gather their own negative energy. Such phrases as "getting out of bed on the wrong side" or "it's all going to Hades in a handbasket" imply that, once set on the wrong course, events head toward an inevitable doom like a snowball gathering mass and speed as it rolls downhill.

In this context, the idea that at any moment you can start again may be a startling one. But it is an idea that is useful when events—like the snowball—seem to be rushing forward, impacting each other, gaining momentum. Starting again involves stopping what you are doing, reflecting, and reminding yourself that it is you—not events—that are in control.

Starting again is like pressing the mental pause button, giving you the chance to be still, to breathe a much longer breath, and to ask yourself, "Can I change what is happening?" When you stop and step out of the situation, you create the opportunity to look back to see where you have come from and how you have gotten there, and then to decide if you have to go where things seem to be heading. This is not a question of going back in time to fix what already has been done, but rather seeing if there is an alternative route, a turnoff from the high-speed path you are on.

It is possible you will decide that you do have to stay on the current course. Nonetheless, pressing the pause button serves the purpose of re-establishing your presence in and awareness of the situation, of letting your mind, heart, and soul catch up with you so that you can proceed in a more conscious and deliberate way.

Whichever path forward you choose, pressing the pause button puts you back in the driver's seat.

Application Exercise

At some time this week when you are in the middle of a situation that seems to be going in a predetermined direction (particularly if it is one you do not like!), take a few moments to stop, press the mental pause button, breathe, ask yourself, and note:

1. What led up to this moment? How did I get here?
2. Is there an alternative route I can take? Can I turn left or right off this road?
3. Do I have to go where this seems to be going?
   If you answer "yes," explain why.
   If you answer "no," list other possible choices.

Remind Yourself

I CAN BEGIN AGAIN AT ANY MOMENT.

Week 46
Expressing Respect

"We like the people who say straight out what they think—provided they think the same as us."
—Mark Twain

FEELING RESPECTED INCLUDES RECOGNITION FROM OTHERS THAT your contribution is appreciated, your expertise is valued, and your character is admired. Undoubtedly this is something we all want. In fact, respect is high on the list of what people say they desire in the workplace.

The difficulty lies in the fact that the expression of respect varies from person to person. I may think I am expressing respect for a person by leaving him alone to work on his job, rather than bothering him with questions about my job. He, however, might think that asking for information or guidance is a way of showing respect and interpret my silence as a gesture of disrespect for what he has to offer.

Much of what we consider to be respectful behavior is based on family upbringing. There are also cultural differences in showing respect. One example involves eye contact. When an American supervisor speaks, she expects her employee to look her in the eyes as a sign of interest and attention. A Japanese employee, however, would show respect to a superior by *not* looking him or her in the eyes.

Seen in this light, expressing respect is more than just using the correct title when addressing a person. It is even more than being polite. It is about taking the extra time to understand a person's position and place in the world as best as you can from where you are. It necessitates stepping out of your own set of expectations to find out those of another. It entails being willing to gently walk into their world, to wear their shoes for a while, and to see the world through their eyes so you can understand their values.

The opposite of this respectful attitude and behavior would be to march into somebody's life with your beliefs, your opinions, your set ways of doing things, and expect them to harmonize with you. Such behavior is based in self-centered insensitivity.

We do not suggest you give up your opinions or ways of doing things. Instead, we recommend you become aware of how you do things and take the time to assess how others prefer to do things. The results of this shift in your awareness and behavior will greatly increase understanding and support between you and your co-workers.

Application Exercise

Find the time this week to speak with at least two of your co-workers about what they consider to be respectful behavior. Your dialogues can cover topics ranging from how they like others to respond when they have done a good job, to their preferences in the use of touch in social interactions. Note how you and your colleagues are the same and how you are different, as well as things that you want to remember when working together. Use the following guide in your notebook:

Co-worker's name:
Ways we are the same:
Ways we are different:
Things to remember when working together:

Remind Yourself

THROUGH AWARENESS, EMPATHY, AND LISTENING,
I SHOW RESPECT FOR THOSE AROUND ME.

Week 47
Increasing Trust

"The misfortune we suffer is seldom, if ever, as bad as that which we fear."
—Johann von Schiller

IN THE ABOVE QUOTE, SCHILLER RECOMMENDS EXPECTING THE best possible outcome. This week we apply that attitude toward people. Expecting the best from people requires teaching yourself to think of others as capable and well-rounded rather than on the basis of what they have done before or how they might appear.

If you have ever worked with someone who did not hold you in very high regard or who thought your capabilities were not up to standard, you know the debilitating effect a lack of trust can have on one's performance. This brings to light how important it is to trust people in their ability to succeed. Even if we do not know whether or not they can come through, giving others a vote of confidence or affirmative praise can help them achieve their best.

Increasing trust does not mean you blindly put yourself into situations where there are clear indications of danger. Nor does it mean that if somebody has betrayed your trust, you have to repeat that same ill-fated action with that person. What is important, however, is to not withhold your sense of trust from *all* people simply because *one* person has disappointed you.

Increasing trust, particularly after it has been broken, entails a series of small, fundamental components. One is to be sure you do not ask for things that are clearly outside the realm of the person's capabilities. Another involves noticing and expressing appreciation for tasks that people perform well, perhaps getting to know them well enough to learn about the kinds of talents they may be expressing outside of the workplace. It is also important to re-establish that you and your co-workers have the same goals and to remember that, as we saw in Week 41, there is more than one right way to do something.

Increasing trust also carries with it a requirement of clear, blame-free, and non-manipulative communication. People can only do what you ask if you have communicated your desire accurately and in a nonthreatening manner. It is important to realize there is a bit of risk-taking in this activity because your request, even if understood, may not be gratified. When that happens, it is important that you not take it personally, but rather to nonjudgmentally seek understanding as to why your request was not fulfilled.

Increasing your ability to trust others brings with it a wonderful feeling of lightness as you walk through the world, knowing that others can support you and help you in your moments of need.

Application Exercise

This week reflect on the following two questions. Write down your thoughts.

1. What does being trusting mean to me?
2. How can I act in a more trusting way?

Remind Yourself

OTHER PEOPLE CAN BE AS TRUSTWORTHY AS I AM.

Week 48
Transforming Conflict

"There is always more good than bad in people, and seeing the good tends to bring it forth."
—Ernest Holmes

CONFLICTS ARISE IN HUMAN INTERACTION. WE ARE ALL DIFFERENT, so it is only natural we would think and act differently. Why is it, then, that so many of us dread and avoid conflict? When a conflict occurs, why do we sometimes go so far as to pretend that it does not exist (which of course only makes it worse)?

One reason we avoid conflict is that we tend to equate disagreeing with someone to disliking them. From this viewpoint, any disagreement can be seen as a personal attack.

Another reason for avoiding conflict is that conflict based in a difference of opinion seems to complicate reaching our work goal, particularly in a fast-paced environment. It appears to be easier and quicker to proceed with one idea—particularly one's own—and not bother to consider other ideas, even when we know we are working toward the same end.

A third reason is that conflict can appear threatening. If someone has an idea different from mine, it raises the possibility that it might be *better* than mine. Therefore, I might feel the need to protect and defend my idea—to prove that I am an intelligent, capable person who has valid ideas.

None of these lines of reasoning is very sound, but they do suggest three ingredients that are essential in transforming conflict.

One is to avoid taking things personally. An idea that is different from mine is just that—*different.* It is not inherently better or worse, just different.

The second ingredient involves looking for the common ground in the opposing ideas. Almost always the apparently differing parties are working toward the same end. Often they are even saying the same thing but in different ways. It is important to consider the opposing viewpoint in terms of how it might help you to achieve your goal.

The third ingredient centers on listening. It is a common reaction in conflict to want to shut down or fight the opposing voice. But in truth we all want to be heard. If we can allow the other person to express him- or herself, and if we can listen with the intent to hear exactly what is being said, there is a good chance the conflict will easily dissipate. Often the perpetuation of conflict occurs not because the ideas are different, but because the ideas are not being fully expressed or understood. It is this very refusal to allow communication to take place that causes the impasse.

Here is an action plan to follow in the event of conflict: listen first; think second; and speak third, and then only to those directly involved, making sure to always focus on *what* is right rather than *who* is right. Above all, remember that conflict is carried out by people whose hearts contain good.

Application Exercise

Bring to mind a recent conflict. Answer the following questions about the conflict:

1. What was the opposing voice saying?
2. Did I allow the other person to be heard?
3. Did I acknowledge the other person?
4. What were we saying that was the same?
5. How would I like to be treated in this situation?
6. Is there a different way I could have been present in this conflict? What would this presence look like?

Remind Yourself

I LISTEN TO DIFFERENT IDEAS WITH AN OPEN MIND AND HEART.

Week 49
Coping with Change

"People wish to be settled:
only as far as they are unsettled, is there any hope for them."
—Ralph Waldo Emerson

HUMAN BEINGS SEEM TO BE AMBIVALENT ABOUT CHANGE.

On the one hand, we crave it. Consider how many new car models appear yearly, how quickly popular music and styles change, how many new products endlessly clamor for our attention, and how much we seek different places for our vacations. Reveling in this aspect of change, Ursula K. LeGuin states: "The only thing that makes life possible is permanent, intolerable uncertainty; not knowing what comes next."

On the other hand, as Emerson points out, there is a part of us that just wants to stay put. Perhaps it is because when we get comfortable we don't like to get up, even though we are bored. Or perhaps we cannot imagine things ever being different, although we long for them to be better. Or perhaps there is a part of us that avoids change simply because we fear we will not "get it right."

Whenever change is afoot—whether we initiate it or it seems to just happen to us—we are dealing with the unknown. We do not know where we are going, how we will respond, what will happen, or how it will all turn out. Change can indeed be unsettling, and coping with change calls upon our courage.

In writing about courage, Walter Anderson notes that worry "doesn't stop the future from unfolding; it only ruins today," and that "courage is acting with fear, not without it." He reminds us that we do not have to be free from all fear before we do the thing that needs doing. He encourages us to make friends with the side of us that avoids change because we know there is another side to us that is courageous and able to take steps—even tiny ones—toward the changes we crave.

Encouragement can also come from reviewing your life path to date. You will probably notice there were times you seemed to be on solid ground, yet in fact it was a series of chaotic changes that got you to that point. You may remember changes that looked ominous at the time but ultimately contained blessings. This reflection brings to light the wisdom in Socrates' advice to remember that "no condition is ever permanent; then you will not be overjoyed in good fortune nor too sorrowful in misfortune."

Application Exercise

Take a few moments this week to answer the following questions in your notebook.

1. What is an example of a change I initiated in my life that led to more good for me?
2. What is an example of an unexpected, seemingly negative change that ultimately contained good?
3. What change would I like to initiate (or respond to) in my life now?
4. Is there any idea, attitude, or belief I need to release in order to initiate (or embrace) this change?
5. What one step can I take this week toward positive change in my life?

Remind Yourself

When change occurs, I have all
I need to create more good in my life.

Week 50
Work as a Stepping Stone

"Think of your work not as a place to make a living but as an opportunity to make a life."
—Eric Butterworth

HUMAN BEINGS HAVE A FUNDAMENTAL NEED TO EXPRESS THEMselves and their unique creativity through their work. When we are doing work that fits our talents and temperament, it becomes a joy, not a drudge. There are many people who feel fulfilled in their jobs. This is an encouraging fact for those of us who are not fulfilled by our jobs, for it provides proof and hope that fulfillment is possible.

Life is always calling us forward to ever greater things. Whether you are a person who enjoys your current job or one who does not, it is important to keep your mind open to the possibility of greater self-expression. As Norman MacEwan points out, "We make a living by what we get, but we make a life by what we give."

History is full of examples of famous people who had surprisingly unrelated jobs. Writer George Orwell spent time as a policeman and a dishwasher. The American composer Charles Ives made his living as an insurance salesman. Physicist Albert Einstein worked in the Swiss patent office. These occupations helped sustain them as they pursued their true passion.

Life also has a way of making sense in retrospect. If you ask someone who is happy in his job about his previous jobs, you will probably hear about an employment history that includes jobs seemingly unrelated to his current one. Yet every job along the way provided skills or character development necessary for the current one.

That is why we invite you this week to consider your job as a stepping stone to doing more of what you love to do. This entails reflecting on what it is you really want to be doing. As this becomes clear, you will be able to see how your current job is helping you on your path. In this way you will be able to more fully appreciate your current job. As you appreciate it more, you will also enjoy it more. For as Eric Butterworth writes in *Spiritual Economics*, "You can change your job, any job, if you change your attitude about it."

Application Exercise

1. In your notebook, list five things that you love to do.
2. Now prioritize them in order of which provide the most vital and enjoyable self-expression.
3. Next to each, make a note of the percentage of time you currently spend doing it.
4. Put a star next to the ones that you would like to do more. Note ideas on how to do this.
5. Now list ways in which your current job is helping you do these things you love.

Remind Yourself

LIFE IS ALWAYS CALLING ME TO A GREATER EXPRESSION OF MYSELF.

Week 51

Listening to Your Intuitive Voice

"Intuition is the discriminating faculty that enables you to decide which of two lines of reasoning is right."
—Paramahansa Yogananda

THIS WEEK WE INVITE YOU TO BEGIN AN ONGOING DISCIPLINE OF listening to your intuitive voice. Intuition is an innate wisdom that has never been disturbed by the ways of the world or the conflict of the workplace. It is a faculty of reason that is on target every time. It expresses as an inner knowing, a calm assured feeling, a voice within that knows the truth.

Many of us do not use this invaluable, ever-present inner resource because it takes time, intention, and practice to develop. Our schedules are often filled with so many things clamoring for our attention that we overlook the first step in developing intuition—giving it time and space.

Another step in developing intuition concerns a shift in awareness. It takes a certain kind of sensitive listening to understand the voice of intuition. We are so used to electronic communications, memos, and newspapers speaking to us in a direct, bold, and linear fashion that we have to practice a "quieter" kind of listening to become aware of our intuition.

Intuition speaks in different ways. It can come to us in thoughts, words, images, sounds, emotions, or physical sensations. It can also come to us in messages from the world around us—a phrase in a book, a line spoken on TV, or a comment from a friend.

When you first begin to seek intuitive guidance, you may be

confused by the different kinds of messages you receive. Some messages may be based on impulse, reaction, or fear, others on the cultural identity you have developed, and still others on the internalized voices of significant people in your life. How can you tell the difference?

Impulse is different from intuition in that impulse typically is a quick reaction to something, whereas intuition involves a calm knowing that remains steadfast over time.

As for differentiating intuition from the voices of fear, cultural identity, and other people, know that your intuitive voice never criticizes. It is never mean-spirited, and it never diminishes you or leaves you feeling sad or unhappy. The intuitive voice always seeks the very best for you because its function in your life is to bring you into harmonious situations.

In the beginning, it may seem difficult to sort out your intuition from other voices. As you practice, though, you will be able to sort through the different personalities of the voices. You will start to recognize a thread weaving through your own authentic intuitive voice. Over time, you can develop your intuition and be able to rely on this internal compass which always points toward more good.

Application Exercise

This week's exercise is an adaptation of a spiritual process known as "visioning," developed by Rev. Dr. Michael Beckwith. It is our hope that, beginning this week, you will be able to use this process to assist you in expanding good in your experience for the rest of your life.

Set aside twenty minutes of uninterrupted time in a space that is as free as possible of distractions. Have your notebook handy, as well as a way to time yourself (perhaps a beeper on a timepiece).

Sitting comfortably in a chair, begin by taking a few deep breaths and relaxing the muscles throughout your face and body. Remind yourself that you have an internal faculty of wisdom that can guide you to greater good in your life.

As you pose each question below, allow yourself at least two minutes of quiet in which your intuition will present you with messages in the form of thoughts, feelings, words, images, or physical sensations. Without judging, simply note what is coming into your awareness.

If your everyday "planning mind" starts to go to work, simply remind yourself that this is a time dedicated to listening for your intuitive voice.

Now, think of a situation for which you would like guidance from your intuition. Ask:

1. What does my intuitive voice have to say about this situation?
   (Allow two minutes of stillness.)
2. What does my intuitive voice tell me about the part I have to play in this situation?
   (Allow two minutes of stillness.)
3. What do I need to release in order for my intuitive voice to guide me successfully in this situation?
   (Allow two minutes of stillness.)
4. What is my next step to reveal more good in this situation?
   (Allow two minutes of stillness.)

When you have posed all the questions and allowed time for answers, write down anything that came to you during this time. Spend a few minutes reflecting on what these things might mean. Note that for some of the things that emerged, the meaning may be obvious. Other things may seem mystifying; like images in a dream, their meaning may become clear over time. Conclude by inviting your intuitive voice to continue to provide you with wisdom and guidance toward right action in this situation.

Remind Yourself

THROUGH INTENTION AND PRACTICE, I DEVELOP MY INNATE WISDOM WHICH GUIDES ME TO WHAT IS BEST FOR ME IN MY LIFE.

Week 52

Your Own Code of Ethical Behavior

"This above all: to thine own self be true, and it must follow, as the night the day, Thou canst not then be false to any man."
—Shakespeare

YOUR *CODE OF ETHICAL BEHAVIOR* IS BOTH YOUR COVENANT and your guide. It is a covenant in that it states your agreement to live according to a set of principles. It is a guide in that it can help you make beneficial decisions—in both simple daily matters as well as major life-altering ones—particularly when other people are pressuring you with their needs. It is a declaration of what you stand for and a reminder to take responsibility for standing for it. It serves as the foundation for living a life of integrity.

To be in integrity means that one's thoughts, words, and actions are in alignment with each other and with one's beliefs and values. To be in integrity means to be in a state of wholeness. When we are out of integrity, we get an uncomfortable feeling (usually referred to as guilt) which points to that place in our life where we need to make an adjustment in order to return to a state of wholeness.

This state of wholeness begins with getting clear on what exactly are your basic values. From this follows the recognition of the kind of behavior that is acceptable and unacceptable to you. This forms the basis for your personal rules of conduct from which you can know what to do and what not to do. Without clarity on these things, it is possible to end up allowing all sorts of unacceptable treatment, action, choices, and behavior to take place in your environment. It becomes possible to lose control and to feel adrift and victimized.

Taking a position on your ethics will help you know whether you are in an environment that supports you. It will also help you create the life you want, for when you get clear on what you stand for, other people will respond to that clarity in you and treat you in a way that aligns with what you stand for.

Simply put, your own *Code of Ethical Behavior* is a statement of what you consider to be good, and what your guidelines are for creating that good in your life.

Application Exercise

This week you will create your personal *Code of Ethical Behavior.* Take time every day this week to reflect on the following statements in Part I. Then write out all the responses to them that come into your head. At the end of the week, review all the ideas you wrote down throughout the week and select the most appropriate ones for you. When you feel comfortable with your selections, write your statements into the corresponding numbered spaces in Part II. This will be your *Code of Ethical Behavior.* You can write this out on a separate piece of paper to hang on the wall or keep in your pocket as a constant guide and companion.

Part I

1. The highest quality in a human being is: (e.g., love, peace, joy, truth, beauty, power, life, light, generosity, kindness, etc.)
2. I am alive in order to:
3. The five most important things for me to do in any situation are: (e.g., tell the truth, express appreciation, share my blessings, etc. If you have more than five, choose the five most crucial ones.)
4. The five things I refuse to do in any situation are: (If you have more than five, choose the five most crucial ones.)
5. My favorite things in life to do are:

Part II

My Code of Ethical Behavior

My life is based in (#1) ________________________________.

I (#2) ____.

I commit to do the following: (#3) ______________________.

I commit to never do the following: (#4) ________________.

I know that good is being expressed in and through me when I do the things I love. Therefore, I commit to spending as much time as possible doing the following: (#5) ______________________.

Remind Yourself

The more I act in integrity, the more good is revealed within and around me.

Recommendations for Seeing More Good

CONGRATULATIONS ON COMPLETING A YEAR OF INCREASING YOUR ability to see and experience good! We have four suggestions for continuing to expand your awareness of good and inviting even more of it into your life.

1. *Do this curriculum again.*

Each time you "re-cycle" through the ideas and activities in this book, they will take on new and expanded meanings. You may remember something you have forgotten, understand something in an entirely new way, or have new challenges to which the concepts can be applied.

2. *Work with supplementary books containing "one-a-day" short readings.*

These books present ideas similar to ours in the form of short daily readings. See Appendix A for suggestions.

3. *Study an inspirational book.*

We are indeed fortunate to be alive at a time when we have access to so much wisdom—contemporary, historical, and ancient. There are so many wonderful books available. See Appendix B for suggestions.

4. *Keep the following statement in your awareness*:
   Good and more Good is mine.
   An ever-increasing Good is mine.
   There is no limit to the Good which is mine.
   Everywhere I go, I see this Good. I feel It, I experience It.
   It crowds itself against me, flows through me, expresses Itself in me, and multiplies Itself around me.

Ernest Holmes wrote these words in *Living the Science of Mind*. He advocated declaring this statement 100 times a day to expand your comprehension and increase your receptivity for good. You may wish to focus on one sentence of the above statement for each day of your five-day workweek, like this:

Monday:	*Good and more Good is mine.*
Tuesday:	*An ever-increasing Good is mine.*
Wednesday:	*There is no limit to the Good which is mine.*
Thursday:	*Everywhere I go, I see Good, I feel It, I experience It.*
Friday:	*Good crowds Itself against me, flows through me, expresses Itself in me, and multiplies Itself around me.*

Appendix A

Books of "One-a-Day" Short Readings

THE FOLLOWING TITLES ARE SOME OF OUR FAVORITE DAYBOOKS. (These authors have also written other books you may enjoy.)

Beckwith, Michael. *40 Day Mind Fast Soul Feast* (Agape, 2000)
Forty short daily readings presenting a mystical view of life.

Boorstein, Sylvia. *It's Easier Than You Think* (Harper SanFrancisco, 1997)
Short, engaging readings presenting ancient Buddhist truths in contemporary terms.

Carlson, Richard. *Don't Sweat the Small Stuff…and it's all small stuff* (Hyperion, 1997)
One hundred "simple ways to keep the little things from taking over your life."

Dean, Amy. *Pleasant Dreams* (Hay House, 2000)
Fifty-two readings inviting more restful nights.

Holmes, Ernest, *365 Science of Mind* (Tarcher/Putnam, 2001)
Daily readings from the author of the classic *The Science of Mind*.

Ryan, M.J. *Attitudes of Gratitude* (Conari Press, 1999)

Sixty-three short readings helping you apply gratitude as a transformative tool.

Shelton, Mary Murray. *Nourishing Thoughts* (Sacred Spiral Press, 1995)

A portable but powerful collection of affirmative statements to help you stay centered through a range of life experiences.

Appendix B
Recommended Inspirational Books

EACH OF THE FOLLOWING BOOKS EXPANDS ON THE IDEAS PRESENTed in *Seeing Good At Work.* Let your intuition guide you as to which book is right for you at the moment. You may want to take a trip to a bookstore and find other titles as well. Many of the authors listed here have written other books. Consider starting a study group to help you apply the ideas presented.

Allen, Marc. *Visionary Business* (New World Library, 1997)
Of particular benefit to those running their own businesses; filled with practical advice based in spiritual law.

Burns, Maureen. *Forgiveness: A Gift You Give Yourself* (Empey Enterprises, 1992)
Provides short readings and exercises to assist in releasing old hurts.

Butterworth, Eric. *Spiritual Economics* 3d ed.(Unity Books, 2001)
Lays a spiritual foundation for understanding and attaining material well-being.

Cameron, Julia. *The Artist's Way* 10th ed.(Tarcher/Putnam, 2002)
Inspirational writing and practical exercises to help you express your unique creative gifts.

Chopra, Deepak. *The Seven Spiritual Laws of Success* (Amber-Allen Publishing, 1995)

Describes and provides exercises for seven guidelines for leading a fulfilling life.

Cole-Whittaker, Terry. *Every Saint Has a Past, Every Sinner a Future* (Tarcher/Putnam, 2001)

Provides the rationale and methods for applying spiritual laws to create a happy and prosperous life.

Easwaran, Eknath. *Your Life Is Your Message: Finding Harmony with Yourself, Others, and the Earth* (Hyperion, 1997)

Discusses how to be more loving, more focused, and better able to live out your ideals, and provides practical spiritual disciplines to bring about these changes.

Hay, Louise. *You Can Heal Your Life* (Hay House, 1984)

Offers spiritual substance and practical exercises to bring healing into all areas of your life.

Holmes, Ernest. *This Thing Called You* (Tarcher/Putnam, 1997/1948)

A poetic and gentle study of the individual's Divine nature .

Johnson, Spencer. *Who Moved My Cheese?* (Putnam, 1998)

An amusing metaphorical story containing wisdom and advice for dealing with change.

Kramer, Jacqueline. *Buddha Mom* (Tarcher/Putnam, 2003)

Applies Buddhist wisdom to family life.

Miller, Fred. *How to Calm Down Even If You're Absolutely, Totally Nuts* (Namaste Press, 1999)

Guidance and techniques to help live life in a more relaxed and present way.

Ruiz, Don Miguel. *The Four Agreements* (Amber-Allen Publishing, 1997)

Powerful, practical, and accessible advice from ancient Toltec wisdom.

Tolle, Eckhart. *The Power of Now* (New World Library, 1999)

Clearly and simply provides the way to understand and lead life from a higher spiritual perspective.

About the Authors

DR. JOYCE DUFFALA has long addressed spirituality in the workplace as a communication trainer for corporations and other organizations. As president of a consulting firm, executive director of a nonprofit organization, and lecturer at the University of San Francisco, University of California/Berkeley and San Francisco State University, she has had ample opportunity to apply what she teaches in her own work life. She is author of *The Teacher as Artist* and coauthor with Mark Rittenberg of *The Active Communicating Survival Kit.*

Raised a Lutheran, Dr. Duffala studied Buddhism for seven years while in residence with the San Francisco Zen Center. A licensed spiritual counselor and guest speaker, she now assists others in realizing more good in their lives.

REV. DR. EDWARD VILJOEN has moved from a career in classical music in South Africa to corporate America, and then to the ministry.

Rev. Dr. Viljoen is Senior Minister at the Santa Rosa Church of Religious Science, where he heads a congregation of over 1,000 people. Through his sermons, classes, workshops, counseling, and media appearances, he makes spiritual principles relevant to a wide range of spiritual seekers. As a Sonoma County Law Enforcement Chaplain, he counsels people from all religious backgrounds.

Rev. Dr. Viljoen is author of *Guide to Reading the Science of Mind in One Year*, published in the Tarcher/Putnam 1998 edition of Ernest Holmes's *Science of Mind*, and has written for *Science of Mind* magazine.